Educational Access and Social Justice

A Global Perspective

Edited by
Gowri Parameswaran and Themina Kader

University Press of America,® Inc.
Lanham · Boulder · New York · Toronto · Plymouth, UK

Copyright © 2009 by
University Press of America,® Inc.
4501 Forbes Boulevard
Suite 200
Lanham, Maryland 20706
UPA Acquisitions Department (301) 459-3366

Estover Road
Plymouth PL6 7PY
United Kingdom

All rights reserved
Printed in the United States of America
British Library Cataloging in Publication Information Available

Library of Congress Control Number: 2008943385
ISBN-13: 978-0-7618-4538-6 (paperback : alk. paper)
eISBN-13: 978-0-7618-4539-3

∞™ The paper used in this publication meets the minimum
requirements of American National Standard for Information
Sciences—Permanence of Paper for Printed Library Materials,
ANSI Z39.48—1984

We dedicate this collection of essays to our parents,
P. Sulochana & P. Parameswaran
The late Abdul A. Karim & Sakina Kaderbhai
who inculcated in us a love of education and
a striving towards social justice

Table of Contents

Preface vii

Introduction ix

I. Public Schooling and Unequal Access to Resources

1. Education in Fiji: Is it Still a Public Service?
    Govinda Ishwar Lingam 3

2. United Arab Emirates' Pre-service Teachers' Attitudes Towards Gifted /Talented Children with Disabilities
    Hala Elhoweris 13

3. 'Poor Girls': A Comparative Analysis Of Their Educational Experiences In England And India
    Mary Thornton and Ponni Iyer 19

4. Access to Education: A Distant Dream for Many in India
    Gowri Parameswaran 31

II. Social Justice Issues in Higher Education

5. Social Justice and Higher Education For All: The Bolivarian University of Venezuela
    Thomas Muhr 43

6. Navigating Art Education Across Three Domains: Cultural, Pedagogical And Political
    Themina Kader 55

7. Out and Abroad: GLBT Resources
    Cory Young

    63

III. Teacher Training and Social Justice

8. Drama and Social Equity in Teacher Education Programs
   In Palestine
      Hala Al-Yamani   77

9. Measuring The Extent To Which Teachers Interpret Their Role In Educational Terms
      Nwachukwu Prince Ololube and Daniel Elemchukwu Egbezor   87

10. Rethinking Equal Voices In Classroom Discourse:
    Arab Female College Students' Views On Literacy Empowerment
       Negmeldin O. Alsheikh   99

About the Authors   107

Preface

It has been eight years since the signing of the 'Education For All' proclamation by the United Nations Educational, Scientific and Cultural Organization in Dakar. The goal of the document was to charge governments around the world with the responsibility to ensure that all children have free access to primary education. Universal literacy for children was to be achieved by 2015. It was unique in that education was declared a universal human right.

For educationists like us who have followed the progress towards these goals by governments around the world, it has been impossible to deny the conclusion that the goal of universal literacy is still a distant dream for the most disadvantaged in the majority of countries. There are just so many barriers for communities trying to provide access to education for their young.

Our project was conceived about two years ago. We wanted scholars from different countries giving us their realities from the ground rather than education researchers based in western universities attempting to capture the status of education in developing countries. The editors also sought manuscript from scholars from various fields within education to give us an understanding of the challenges and rewards for children in mastering different areas of educational achievement.

The result has been a multi-layered, and inter-disciplinary set of articles on the special issues surrounding educating our youth and children for the demands of the 21st century. From occupied Palestine to a large democracy like India, governments, NGOs, educationists and advocacy groups are sometimes confronting and sometimes being co-opted by privileged special interests. As we plod along towards universal access to education, the diversity of educational needs and demands dictate specific actions and pedagogies that educationists adopt.

The editors are immensely pleased with the final collection of essays and would like to thank all the contributors for sticking with this endeavor even when we seemed to not be going anywhere. The authors would like to thank our parents most for valuing knowledge and encouraging us to do the same.

Gowri Parameswaran and Themina Kader
New Paltz, July 2008

Introduction

The United Nations and western nations in recent years have identified education as a great progressive force in the world with infinite potential to change the lives of individuals and nations for the better. There have been numerous studies conducted in developing countries that show that women who are educated have fewer children, earn more, are more assertive in their relationships with their spouses and typically have better quality of life than women who are illiterate. Thus access to education has been touted as the great equalizer in the modern world and is a human right that all individuals should enjoy.

UNESCO estimates that nearly one billion people in the world are illiterate. The Education For All (EFA) goals, that were reaffirmed at the Dakar World Education Forum in 2000, were unusual in recognizing the right to education as a basic human right: The final declaration of the Dakar conference charged governments around the world with the task of ensuring that by 2015 all children will have access to and complete free and compulsory primary education of good quality'.

In order to achieve this grand target, the EFA goals were deliberately discussed in general terms and the specific path towards universal literacy was left up to individual communities and governments. None of the individual goals is stand-alone by itself and all of the goals involve increasing access to primary and higher education as well as improving the quality of the curriculum and training of instructors who deliver these educational services. Most of all, values of equality and social justice were to be the guiding principles of everything that governments and non-governmental agencies did.

It has been eight years since the EFA declaration was made in Dakar. Yet the reality is that the majority of the countries monitored have only marginally reduced the numbers of the illiterate in their countries. Eighty million children and almost a billion adults still do not receive any education, even an inadequate one, according to the 2007 EFA Global Monitoring Report (GMR). The least economically developed countries are overrepresented in the group that has a disproportionately large number of people without access to schooling.

The importance of easy access to elementary and early child hood education is emphasized by the primacy of the goals in the list of EFA goals arrived at in Dakar; it is also echoed again in the Millennium Development Goals as conceived by the UN. Child development experts acknowledge that the earlier children are taught to read, write and listen, the faster they learn, and the bigger the return on the investment, to society. An examination of access to early childhood care and education (ECCE) reveals that most families in poverty cannot afford services that require payment.

The problem of inequitable access to education is made more serious by the severe lack of qualified teachers who are sensitive to issues of social justice or who come from underrepresented and disadvantaged communities. UNESCO estimates that the increased demand for teachers under EFA and the high rates of retirement of older teachers will create a dire situation for children in terms of their access to education. A related issue is the lack of female teachers in traditional communities, which makes it difficult to achieve gender parity in educational attainment.

In a world that is increasingly intertwined, and with globalization and trade rules that favor the wealthy both within the developing world and in the relationship of third world nations with wealthy nations, education has effectively divided the haves from the have-nots. This collection of essays studies the particular contexts within which these inequities manifest themselves and their implications for members of that particular society. Some of the articles analyze and describe who is invited and who is left out to partake of this valuable social commodity. Other articles outline lessons learned, as communities prove successful or fail in their efforts to open up pathways to democratic citizenship and civic participation for all segments of their populations.

The book is divided into three major sections, each section dealing with different elements of access to educational opportunities and the implications of existing inequality on student learning, especially in marginalized communities

The first section, titled public schooling and social equity, has four articles that enumerate the problem of universal access to education in developing countries as well as by marginalized groups in the USA. Govinda explores the problem of the increasing privatization of education in Fiji as it undergoes enormous economic transformations and increasing affluence. The government of Fiji has not changed the proportion of its economic wealth on education, especially among children who are disadvantaged. The privileged in society has used the current political turmoil in Fiji to repress the demands of the marginalized. Unless the poor and the disadvantaged have access to resources, the current instability will worsen. Hala Elhoweris examines the invisibility of the disabled in a traditional country like the United Arab Emirates. While the government spends a large proportion of its GDP on education, very little of it is allocated to the education of the mentally and the physically challenged students. They are invisible and have few avenues for self-fulfillment or independence. Thornton and Iyer examine the status of poor girls in schools in both India and England and find it wanting. They examine the double-disadvantage that poverty and gender raises for girls in their quest for education. They suggest ways in which governments can help address the educational deficits that poor girls face. Parameswaran outlines the history of Dalit (untouchable) oppression in India and the challenges that proponents of social justice face in ensuring availability of basic educational access to members of the lowest rung of the caste hierarchy.

The second major section of the book, social justice issues in higher education, deals with who has access to the privilege of higher education in a variety of contexts and the impact it has on the rest of society in a country. In Thomas Muhr's essay, he analyzes the strategic role of Higher Education For All (HEFA) in realizing social justice in the Bolivarian Republic of Venezuela. Through case study experiences, he illustrates the vast potential of the transdisciplinary study programs consisting of both students and community members where participants learn to co-create public policies and solve problems that affect them locally. Kader examines art education across three domains—the social/cultural, the pedagogical/experiential and the religious/political. She observes and parses issues of agency pertaining to and the rights and privileges of the marginalized populace of the non-Western art world, the anti-Islamic attitudes currently prevailing in western teaching schools, and the biased and faulty information imparted in the name of multicultural art education in the west. Young addresses the important issue of the invisibility of homosexual students both in public schools as well as in higher education in the west. Young draws conclusions from her own study with international students about what topics a program that explores sexual orientation should teach and their social, political and religious impact.

The final section deals with teacher training and social justice. Yamani examines pre-service and in-service teachers' narratives in Palestine as they learn to do self-conscious reflection through drama and play. Many of these teachers and their students live in an exceedingly violent context and drama enables them to explore thorny issues and transform their teaching into one that enables positive social action. Ololube and Egbezor examine attitudes of teachers in Nigeria, a country with the high achievement levels among its student population. He analyzes the various components of their relationship with their students and the dimension that most relate to student success. He also examines the role that teacher job satisfaction plays in increasing student achievement. His findings are related to teacher training and the importance of introducing appropriate skills and dispositions that are invaluable for future teachers. Finally, Al Sheikh explores the role that gender and culture plays in the UAE among women enrolled in teacher training courses. The study enumerated the relation between the subjective-self and the social objectivity by looking at classroom discourse as it generates consciousness through social practices.

In conclusion, the current collection of essays on the issue of educational access and social justice portrays a series of local contexts within an interconnected world, increasingly polarized and unequal, and the role that education plays within individual societies in either equalizing the playing field for the different populations, or in increasing the divide between the privileged and the marginalized.

Public Schooling and
Unequal Access to Resources

Education in Fiji: Is it Still A Public Service?

Govinda Ishwar Lingam
University of the South Pacific, Suva, Fiji

Historical Background

Fiji is known officially as the Republic of the Fiji Islands. It is in the South Pacific and is made up over 300 islands covering a land area of about 194,000 square kilometers. The most remote island is Rotuma, which is about 400 kilometers away from the capital city, Suva. Most of the islands are scattered, thus geographically separate and isolated. According to the 2007 census, Fiji has a population of about 827,900 consisting of two major ethnic groups, Fijians and Indo-Fijians, and several other significant minority groups, such as Rotumans, Chinese, and the Banabans. The Indo-Fijians are mainly the descendants of the indentured labourers who were brought from India by the British in the late 19th Century to provide labor for the sugar industry. Fiji's annual population growth rate is about 1 per cent (Fiji Ministry of Education, 2000). According to Bray, (1991) a country with a population not exceeding 1.5 million, and with limited financial resources, is considered a small country. It faces difficulties in meeting competing demands of various sectors of the economy, exacerbated by continued political instability that has been going on for over two decades. This has had an adverse effect on an already weak economy that relies heavily on tourism and agriculture, the main source of foreign exchange, with implications for the development of all sectors of the economy, particularly education.

Education plays a vital role in the development of an individual and, in turn, of a nation. Good quality education for all the citizens is a pre-condition for a better nation. In Fiji, the disadvantaged sections of the community, who come from lower socioeconomic backgrounds, deserve greater attention than those who can afford the rising costs of educating their children. If children miss out on education, especially basic education, then they are likely to face more challenges in securing a better livelihood and a good future for themselves. Seen in this light, education is a critical factor in any nation's progress and development.

For much of Fiji's independent history, since 1970, the country has been through four coups that have had a negative impact on socio-economic development (Ministry of Education, 2000). For example, the expiry of land leases has led to the displacement of mainly sugar cane farmers with the result that some of the schools in the farming communities are now serving a smaller student population than before. However, support from overseas aid donors such as the Australian Agency for International Development and the European Union have contributed to the advancement of education, in Fiji. This political instability, notwithstanding, there is a rising demand for schooling due to the growing economic importance attached to education as a source of skilled manpower (Thomas and Postlethwaite, 1984). As a result, a number of schools were set up throughout the country, especially in the more remote islands, to provide easy access for school-age children.

Education in Fiji

In the Fijian context, schools can trace their origin, and still owe their existence to the initiatives of Catholic and the Methodist missions, and later to various socio-religious organizations. Some of the socio-religious organizations are the Sanatan Dharam Pratinidhi Sabha, the Arya Pratinidhi Sabha, the former India Sanmarga Ikya Sangam, the Fiji Sikh Society, the Gujarat Society of Fiji and the Fiji Muslim League. In addition to these, a number of school 'committees', which represent a locality or an interested group of people or association, were responsible for the setting up of schools. As pointed out in the 1969 Education Commission Report,

> "The history of education in Fiji is largely one of private initiative and effort. It appears that the main reason for this unusual state of affairs is that the thirst for education, among the communities has consistently outstripped the Government's ability to satisfy it. Consequently, the various Christian missions and more recently various other religious and secular organizations have stepped into the breach." (p. 6)

Furthermore, the Compulsory Education Order of 1997 has led to an increase in school age children attending primary school on a regular basis giving rise to the establishment of more schools in post-independent Fiji. Hence, even in the remotest settlement there is a school and teachers are the only civil servants found there. At the present moment, the majority of the schools, both primary and secondary, are owned and run by non-governmental organizations. Table I shows the different controlling authorities that own and run both primary and secondary schools in Fiji

This has been an on-going trend and has gathered momentum rather than diminished. Primary education has achieved an impressive level of enrollment that clearly demonstrates the parents' concern for the education of their children.

Table 1: Controlling authorities of schools in Fiji

Controlling Authorities	Primary	Secondary
Committees	529	73
Religious Organizations	130	54
Cultural organizations	36	11
Special Education Societies	14	-
Private	4	1
Fijian Affairs Board	-	1
Rabi Council	-	1
Rotuma Council	-	1
Government	2	12
Total	715	154

Source: Tavola, 2000 a, pp. 27-28.

State Intervention

Even though most schools are run by non-government organizations, they are still coordinated by the Ministry of Education whose policies are considered discriminatory. Various professional matters such as curriculum development and examinations are also centralized, and as such come under the jurisdiction of the Ministry of Education. With regard to teaching, all schools follow a fairly uniform curriculum. Generally, the government is responsible for the preparation of teachers, and upon receiving their professional certification the Ministry of Education appoints them and also pays their salaries. At the primary school level, the government provides per capita grants to facilitate free primary education. Table 2 indicates the fee-free grants to primary schools that are based on student population. Although, the fee-free grants were put in place in 1994, not all school age children attended school, because for parents the grant monies did not alleviate the financial burden of high inflationary trends and rising cost of living. Hence the introduction of a Compulsory Education Order to ensure that all school age children did attend school.

Table 2: Fee-free grants to primary schools (F$)

Schools with 10 to 49 pupils	$3,500 p.a. per school
Schools with 50 to 99 pupils	$4,000 p.a. per school
Schools with 100 to 149 pupils	$4,500 p.a. per school
Schools with over 150 pupils	$30 per pupil per year

Source: Tavola, 2000 a, p. 26.

Fee-free grant has been gradually extended to the senior secondary level with a slightly different structure. The government contributes building grants, and gives remission of fees to needy children, in grades 11 and 12, whose parents' income is less than F$5,000 per annum. The assistance provided to these children is shown in Table 3.

Table 3: Remission of Fees for Forms 5 and 6

	Remission of Fees	
Parental income	Tuition	Boarding
$500 or less	$120	$80
$501 to $1,500	$80	$63
$1,501 to $3,500	$40	$27
$3,501 to $5,000	$40	$27

Source: Bacchus, 2000, pp. 441-467.

Despite the per capita grant for tuition fees, schools continue to levy additional fees, for sports, stationery, buildings, examinations, and admission. For example, a school can charge students F$30 for Building; F$5 for Sports; F$35 for Stationery; F$5 for Miscellaneous items; F$10 for Term One, F$10 for Term Two; and F$10 for Term Three. More recently, The Fiji Teachers' Union expressed concern over the issue of school fees. The General Secretary of the Union stated that there were some schools which were charging as much as $600 as annual fees for Form Seven students (Singh, 2007). The Union claims that school administration takes advantage of a system in which no guidelines are set for fees charged. Apart from school fees, parents have to meet other indirect costs of sending their children to school in the form of bus fares, stationery, excursions, uniforms and also contribute towards school fund-raising activities. The latter activity puts a lot of pressure on parents and teachers alike. Students and teachers spend valuable time organizing carnivals, bazaars, lotteries, walkathons, tuck-shops and the like to raise funds for development projects as well for the day to day running of the school. School managements believe that the amount they receive from the Ministry of Education is insufficient to run their schools because of the escalating cost of living

Non-government Efforts

As can be seen from the preceding section, education in Fiji is not a public service in the true sense. An outstanding feature in education is the ownership of schools, with a large number of schools established and run by non-government organizations. At present, the Ministry of Education, for instance, runs only two primary schools, the rest being progressively handed over to various communities to manage. Likewise, at the secondary level only 11 of the 154 schools are owned and run by the government. For these schools the government is responsible for their recurrent and capital expenditure. In this regard, the Ministry of Education's role is purely a facilitative one in partnership with various other stakeholders of education, besides its coordinating role through educational policy development, supervision and partial funding.

Currently, non-government providers of education have generally responded well in meeting the educational needs of the nation's school age children. Different communities have increasingly pinned their hopes on the education of their children, in the belief that success in education can enhance life choices and in turn lead to a secure livelihood. In doing so, communities have made sacrifices to contribute positively to most school development projects. The continuing partnership between the government and non-government organizations in providing education is certainly encouraging. However, when one delves deeply into certain policies of the government, it can be seen that certain sections of the community are marginalized because it appears that the government is taking advantage of this partnership. While this partnership may reduce government's financial burden, the financial contribution by the low-income earners of the communities is considered a 'real' burden. For example, the Fiji Poverty Report pointed out that of the large number of people living in poverty, two thirds were in rural areas and the other third in urban areas (Bacchus, 2000). Education of children of those parents living in poverty is of concern as they will continue to be adversely affected.

Disadvantaged Communities and Schools

Poverty is a major factor restricting the opportunities for good education of children from disadvantaged backgrounds. The recent Fiji Islands Education Commission report pointed out that, "there are inevitably many children who are handicapped by poverty in their educational endeavors" (Tavola, 2000b, p. 265). Disadvantaged families cannot make a living, let alone send their children to school. This has an adverse impact on the education of children from low-income families. The hardships faced by such sections of the population are of great concern and warrant government attention and political will to remedy the problem.

The idea of equal opportunity for all in education in Fiji is thus a myth. The elite can afford the best educational institutions in the country, whereas the poor have to choose either second or third class institutions for their children. For example, small rural schools, remote from administrative centers, are generally the last ones to receive attention from the Ministry of Education and the government. In such remote areas, parents have to sacrifice whatever limited resources they have for the education of their children. In particular, low-income parents in contemporary Fiji cannot meet the increasing costs of educating their children, even though it is tuition-free. The Fiji Poverty Report (UNDP, 1997) highlighted that around 25 per cent of the households earned about F$4316 a year. With this income, it is difficult for most parents to send more than one child to school. Furthermore, where the school is far away from home, it poses further difficulties, as more expenses are incurred.

Schools in low-income communities have generally poor resources and as a result are considered inferior to those in towns and cities. Statistics show that

78.7 per cent of primary schools are in rural areas and, of these, 385 are in very remote areas; 51.9 per cent of secondary schools are in rural areas, out of which 23.7 per cent are in very remote areas (Tavola, 2000a). School buildings in most rural locations are sub-standard, needing maintenance. Since the communities running these schools are economically poor, they find it extremely difficult to maintain school buildings and facilities. Also, the government's fee-free grant policy based on student population is another disadvantage small rural schools have to confront. Consequently, such schools are under-resourced and in turn provide limited opportunities for children's success in education. Rural children's basic education is thus an area of great concern. A report on social justice in Fiji has this to say about the quality of education for rural and urban children:

> "Disadvantage is not simply a question of numbers. Even if rural children had the same statistical chance of going to school as urban children, their access would not be equal if the quality of the schooling was consistently and significantly inferior to that of urban children; they would be disadvantaged." (Ghai & Jill, 2000, p. 10).

In this regard, a report on education in Fiji labeled rural schools as the *Cinderella of the education system* (Barr, 1990, p. 108), perpetuating persistent inequality of opportunity in education because children of disadvantaged sections of the population cannot afford to 'buy' good education. Therefore, from a 'social market' perspective, 'school curriculum' is the commodity, and children the consumers to be embedded with knowledge and skills by teachers who perform a service function.

As mentioned earlier, the curriculum is centrally developed and the interests of the elite or the dominant group supersede the interests of all other groups, especially those living in rural areas. Lack of flexibility in the curriculum makes it unsuitable for people in all parts of the country. According to Hopkins (1997), "this implied view of curriculum is that of a commodity to be dispensed to students" (p. 70). It is rather unfortunate that not all children have full benefits to consume the commodity. Similarly, the recent education commission report pointed out that schools located in disadvantaged areas face other difficulties, such as lack of basic resources for teaching and learning and this makes teachers' work difficult to promote academic achievement among their students (Tavola, 2000c). Students drop out of schools early without completing full primary or secondary education. Due to their plight, many disadvantaged communities fail to take schooling seriously.

Special Funding Assistance

Special funding assistance implemented under the recent *affirmative action program* by the government to help bridge the 'education gap' between ethnic Fijians and Indo-Fijians is problematic. The latter is specifically designed to benefit the children of one ethnic group, over another. Only those schools, which are managed and run by indigenous Fijians, are entitled for state assistance. However, in examining student enrolment in Indo-Fijian schools, it turns out that some of these schools have a high enrolment of indigenous Fijian students. Under the affirmative action policy, these schools do not qualify for state assistance, even though they have a high composition of indigenous Fijian students. Also children of other ethnic groups enrolled in these schools deserve state assistance as they come from poor families. The document on the *Blueprint for Affirmative Action on Fijian Education* states that "a minimum standard for school facilities and maintenance is to be set for all Fijian schools by the Government" (Fiji Ministry of Education, 2000, p. 9).

In Fiji, the affirmative action plan is based on ethnicity and neglects other important considerations of gender, social class, and location of school age children. Social justice is enshrined in the Fiji constitution and the Social Justice Essay of the constitution has provisions to put in place programs to assist individuals or disadvantaged sections of the population to achieve equality of opportunity in education. However, bearing in mind the nature of Fiji's multicultural community, an affirmative action plan based on ethnicity does not augur well for social justice and equity in education. When one looks at the statistics related to people living in poverty, one realizes that they comprise people from all ethnic backgrounds. In the rural areas statistics show that the landless laborers who are mostly Indo-Fijians, are the poorest (Bacchus, 2000). This has implications for the education of Indo-Fijian children and other minority groups living in Fiji. What is there in place for these children and those indigenous Fijian children in multiracial schools? Quality education offered by schools is important for **all** children and not just for a particular ethnic group. Rather than polarize the school system, the government-backed affirmative action program should cater for the education of all disadvantaged children, irrespective of ethnicity. That is to say, governments should provide assistance to schools on the basis of need rather than on the basis of school management. As it is, the present affirmative action policy is discriminatory. As far back as colonial times, the government in Fiji had failed to provide equal opportunities for all in education. The government at that time gave two pounds for the education of European children, 50 pence for Fijian children and 20 pence for Indian children (Sharma, 1989). The policy of differential educational opportunities on the basis of ethnicity is unjust and further marginalizes the disadvantaged sections of the population as well as breeding racial discrimination. To bring about appropriate changes in the educational scene here in Fiji, political as well as public awareness is warranted. In particular, political and educational leaders at all levels, especially higher education, need to find ways to make education an elementary investment for the nation's children.

Conclusion

It is natural for all parents to hope for and try to secure a bright future for their children by sending them to good schools. Through education they can improve their cultural and material well-being. However, in Fiji education at the present time operates within the framework of a market ideology and this adversely affects disadvantaged groups. Parents from these groups are not in a financial position to secure a bright future for their children. Not only do they lack financial resources, but also right 'contacts'. In this respect, children in the top social strata stand a better chance of attending prestigious institutions and in turn opportunities for lucrative employment. If education in Fiji is to be regarded truly as an important public service, then it should be the government's top priority to see that it is available to all, no matter where they live. Otherwise provision of education to as wide a section of the population as possible at an affordable cost may remain a continuing challenge leading to ever-increasing disparities in Fiji. Educational leaders and other partners can and should play a key role in the enhancement of education for all disadvantaged sections of the population.

References

Bacchus, K. 2000. "A Review of the Social and Economic Features of Fiji's Society as they affect Education" In Learning Together: Directions for Education in Fiji Islands. Fiji: Government Printer.

Barr, K. 1990. Poverty in Fiji: Fiji Forum for Justice, Peace and the Integrity of Creation. Fiji: Suva. 108.

Bray, M. 1991. Ministries of Education in Small States: Case Studies of Organization and Management. Commonwealth Secretariat: University of Hong Kong.

Fiji Education Commission. 1969. Education for Modern Fiji. Suva, Fiji: Government Printer.

Fiji Ministry of Education, 2000. Blueprint for Affirmative Action on Fijian Education Suva, Fiji: Ministry of Education.

Ghai, Y. and Jill, C. 2000. Social Justice and Affirmative Action: A Report to the Government of the Fiji Islands on a National Plan for Affirmative Action Under Essay 5 of the Constitution. Fiji: Government Printer.

Hopkins, D. 1997. "Making sense of change" In Educational Management: Strategy Quality and Resources, edited by Preedy M, Glatter R and Levacic Rin Buckingham: Open University Press.

Sharma, A. 1989. "Multicraft in Fijian Secondary Schools: An Evaluative Study of a Non-formal Education Programme". M. Ed. Thesis, University of New England

Singh, A. 2007. "Money barrier to Form Seven," The Sunday Times, May 20, 2007.

Tavola, H. 2000a. "Status Report" In Learning Together: Directions for Education in Fiji Islands. Fiji: Government Printer.

_____, 2000b. "Education and The Economically Disadvantaged" In Learning Together: Directions for Education in Fiji Islands. Fiji: Government Printer.

_____, 2000c. "Education in Rural Fiji" In Learning Together: Directions for Education in Fiji Islands. Fiji: Government Printer.

Thomas, R. M. and Postlethwaite, T. N. 1984. Schooling in the Pacific Islands. New York: Pergamon Press.

UNDP. 1997. Fiji Poverty Report. Suva, Fiji: UNDP.

United Arab Emirates Pre-service Teachers' Attitudes Towards Gifted/Talented Children with Disabilities

Hala Elhoweris
United Arab Emirates University, UAE

Introduction

The major purpose of this study was to examine the influence that the labels Learning Disabled (LD) and Behavioral Disorder (BD) have on United Arab Emirates pre-service teachers regarding their recommendations for referral and placement of gifted students.

Although it is generally accepted in the United Arab Emirates (UAE) that gifted students are those who have potential ability or demonstrate high ability in several areas such as intellectual, creative, specific academic or leadership ability in the performing and visual arts, limited empirical data are available regarding the definition of giftedness in the UAE. Defining giftedness becomes very important when the definition determines who will be included or excluded from the gifted and talented programs.

Many people have difficulties comprehending that a child can be gifted and also have a disability. Identifying students for gifted programs and individuals with disabilities for special education services tend to be mutually exclusive activities. As a result, children with special needs are rarely identified as gifted and talented and are often poorly served. Indeed, gifted children with disabilities are recognized only for their disability, not for their gifts and talents. Thus, they are much less likely than non-disabled gifted children to be identified as gifted and included in school programs that help develop their special talents (Davis and Rimm, 2004, p. 378).

One of the most serious problems plaguing the field of gifted education is the under-representation of students with disabilities in gifted and talented programs. Although the Jacob K. Javits Gifted and Talented Students Act of 1988 provides financial assistance to state and local educational agencies in the U.S. and gives highest priority to students from diverse ethnic backgrounds, economically disadvantaged, limited English proficient, and students with disabilities, the under-representation of students with disabilities in gifted and talented program still persists in the U.S. (Davis and Rimm, 2004, 272-397).

Most schools around the world still base their identification of gifted students on high general intelligence as measured by group or individual intelligence tests and high achievement test scores (Piirto, 2007, 180-250). As a result, access to gifted programs continues to be limited for many students who do not perform well on these measures. Previous research also shows that the traditional identification procedures, negative stereotyping, and lack of sensitivity to cultural variations in the demonstration of special abilities, have greatly contributed to the disparity in this area of enrichment opportunities (Maker, 1996, 42-50). Since several school districts around the world (Davis and Rimm, 2004) include teachers' nomination as part of their selection criteria, teachers tend to be the primary source of determining who will be included or excluded in the gifted and talented programs. Whether or not teachers are qualified to identify gifted and talented students has been the topic of much debate throughout the years (Hoge & Cudmore, 1986, 181-196; Renzulli, 1979). While research appears to support the use of teachers' ratings of student behaviors (Renzulli, 1979; Renzulli, 1978, 180-184; Rohrer, 1995, 269-283), there is also a body of research that suggests that certain biases exist when rating students (Gagné, 1993, 69-77; Siegle 2001).

Indeed, research in the U.S. and elsewhere has shown that teachers are much more likely to refer non-disabled students than students with learning disabilities for placement in gifted and talented programs. For instance, Minner (1990, 37-39) discovered that when teachers studied near-identical vignettes of children, schoolteachers were less likely to identify for gifted and talented programs those who were described as having a learning disability. Additionally, Davis and Rimm (2004, 380-381) indicated that many gifted children with emotional disturbances are not identified as gifted, and do not participate in the U.S. gifted programs.

Researchers such as Minner, 1990 and Elhoweris, 2008 who investigated the effects of disability labels on teachers' perceptions and expectations for students with disabilities, document that both pre-service and in-service teachers hold lower expectations for students with disabilities, and were less likely to identify for gifted and talented programs those who were described as having a learning disability. In Minner's study teacher expectations were influenced by the child's disability category and that these expectations cause the teacher to interact with students with and without disability differently. Moreover in a more recent study, Elhoweris found that, when making referrals to gifted and talented programs, labels such as learning disability, physical disability, and behavioral disorder significantly influenced teachers. More specifically, both general and special education teachers were much less willing to place students with disability labels in gifted and talented programs.

Overall, research in the U.S. and elsewhere indicates that assessment of giftedness influenced by cultural mores associated with disability results in low referral rates of disabled students for gifted and talented programs (Davis & Rimm, 2004, 378-389). Identifying gifted children with disabilities is difficult. A major problem is that their gifts usually remain invisible to teachers. Much of the difficulty for some educators has been the misguided concept that "learning disabilities" and "giftedness" occur at opposite ends of the learning spectrum (Davis & Rimm, 2004, 378-388). However, a strong body of literature now supports the existence of both conditions existing simultaneously.

While attention has focused on teachers' identification practices with culturally diverse youth in gifted and talented programs in the UAE, there is paucity of empirical research examining the effect of the child's disability category on teachers' referral and placement decisions of gifted and talented children in the UAE. The particular focus of this study, therefore, is to examine the influence that the labels learning disabled (LD) and behavioral disorder (BD) have upon pre-service teachers' referral and placement decisions of gifted and talented children.

Method

Participants

The participants of this study consisted of 144 pre-service undergraduate female students enrolled in the College of Education at the United Arab Emirates University. The average age of the participants was 22 years old. The majority of the participants (61%) specialized in elementary education; 33% of the participants specialized in special education, and 6% reported that their area of specialization was early childhood education. One hundred and thirty one pre service teachers (91%) had not taken any course in gifted education.

Procedures

All participants were assigned randomly to treatment conditions and told that the investigator was interested in how pre-service teachers perceived gifted youngsters. Each group was presented then with a survey instrument that contained a short vignette describing a gifted child. All vignettes were identical except for the disability category of the child.
Group 1, the vignette described a fourth grader with learning disability
Group 2, the vignette described a fourth grader with behavioral disorder. Group 3, was the control group in which the vignette provided no information on a fourth grader's student's disability category. Immediately after reading the descriptive vignette, pre-service teachers responded to the two questions. Specifically, participants were asked if they would refer the student for possible placement in a gifted program and if they would recommend that the student be

placed in a gifted program. Each question was followed by a six point Likert Scale. The reading of the vignette and the scale took approximately 15 minutes to complete.

Instrumentation

A short descriptive vignette about a student who should be placed in a gifted program was developed because of the information it revealed in relation to the goal of this study. To ensure content validity, all the traits in the vignette were derived from descriptions of gifted children in introductory special education textbooks by Piirto (2007, 260-280) and Davis and Rimm (2004, 32-53). The content validity was assessed also by sending a copy of the instrument (case vignette) to three experts in the field of gifted education. Each expert assessed the intended content area. The test-retest reliability for the two questionnaire items was adequate for the purpose of this study ($r = .75$, $p < .05$; $r = .76$, $p < .05$).

Results

Data were analyzed using analysis of variance (ANOVA) procedure on the two items. The analysis of the first question, the teachers' initial willingness to refer the described student for a comprehensive evaluation, revealed that significant differences ($F = 24$; $p. .05$) existed depending upon the label appended to the child. The post-hoc analysis [Scheffe technique] indicated that the pre-service teacher's initial willingness to refer the non-labled child (mean = 3.72) significantly differed from their willingness to refer the LD student (mean = 3.33) and the BD student (mean = 2.97).

The second item assessed the pre-service teachers' recommendation decisions to place the described student in a program for gifted youngsters. Again a significant difference ($F = 47$, $p .05$) existed dependent upon the labeled condition of the student. The post-hoc test revealed that teachers were found to be more likely to refer the non labeled gifted student (mean = 3.51) than the LD student (mean= 3.0) and the BD student (mean = 2.13).

Since all the participants were females and the majority of them had not taken any class in gifted education before and their age group is almost the same, data were only analyzed in relation to the participants' area of specialization. No differences existed on the basis of the participants' area of specialization.

Discussion

A significant difference regarding both the referral and placement decisions was found between the control group and the other two groups (LD, BD). The results of this study indicated that labels have an initial negative effect upon pre-service teachers' referral and placement recommendations in the gifted programs. Teachers were more likely to refer the non-labeled student for the gifted/talented program than to refer the LD student and the BD student. Additionally, pre-service teachers were prone to place the child in the gifted/talented program based on the label appended to the student; on the other hand, the same teachers tended to place the non-labeled student in gifted and talented program than to place the labeled students (LD and BD).

The findings of this study indicated that the child's disability category has an effect on pre-service referral and placement recommendations in the gifted and talented program. This result is consistent with Minner's findings (1990, 37-39) that proved that when teachers studied near-identical vignettes of children, they were less likely to identify for gifted and talented programs those who were described as having a learning disability.

It is evident from this study that pre-service teacher expectations regarding disability were strong when pre-service teachers treated the identical information contained in the case vignettes differently. The potential negative bias found in the present study toward children with learning disabilities and behavioral disorders is unfortunate as learning disabled and behavioral disorder children make up the majority of school children in the United Arab Emirates special education classrooms.

The fact that pre-service teachers are much less willing to place a gifted LD student and BD student in a gifted program or even refer these students for evaluation is disturbing. It has been recommended that to reduce the inappropriate and biased referrals to programs for students with disabilities and to increase the number of appropriate referrals to programs for gifted and talented students, regular educators' knowledge of the contextual, cultural, gender, and socioeconomic factors should be increased (Gay, 2000, 22-42).

Extensive research also documents the far-reaching effects of teacher expectations on the performance of children and how teachers' beliefs can be changed. What teachers expect of students influences what students come to expect of themselves. Therefore, teacher education programs should focus on changing teachers' attitude toward children with disabilities. Research demonstrated that attitudes of pre-service teachers can be positively influenced by an academic course in which using individuals with a disability as guest speakers, who can talk about their successful experiences and explain how they compensate for their disability, can be a good strategy to promote positive attitudes toward individuals with disabilities (Salend, 2005, 208-240). Additionally, teacher education programs should all available resources such as films and videos of gifted children with disabilities to promote positive attitudes toward individuals with disabilities.

Interestingly, the area of specialization does not make any difference in pre-service teachers' decisions. Special and general education pre-service teachers were generally unwilling to consider referring or placing a child with a disability in a Gifted/Talented program. Since United Arab Emirates University requires all education majors to take a course on student with disabilities, more courses on diversity may need to be offered. Indeed, the solution to this problem rests in providing more training at pre-service level in multicultural education to meet the needs of gifted students with disabilities.

References

Elhoweris, Hala. 2009. The effect of the child's disability on United Arab Emirates inservice teachers' educational decisions of gifted and talented children. *Educational Studies*. Vol 35, 2.

Gagné, Francoys. 1993. Sex differences in the aptitude and talents of children as judged by peers and teachers. *Gifted Child Quarterly*, 37: 69-77.

Gary, Davis, and Rimm Sylvia. .2004. *Education of the gifted and talented*. Boston: Allyn and Bacon.

Gay, Geneva. 2000. *Culturally responsive teaching: Theory, research, practice.* Columbia University: Teacher College Press.

Hoge, Robert and Cudmore. 1986. The use of teacher-judgment measures in the identification of gifted pupils. *Teaching and Teacher Education, 2:* 181-196.

Maker, June. 1996. Identification of gifted minority students: A national problem, needed changed and a promising solution. *Gifted Child Quarterly, 40* (1): 42-50.

Minner, Sam. 1990. Teacher evaluations of case descriptions of LD gifted children. Gifted Child Quarterly, 34(1): 37-39.

Piirto, Jane. 2007. *Talented Children and Adults: their development and education.* Columbus, OH: Merrill.

Renzulli, Joseph. 1979. *What makes giftedness: A reexamination of the definition of the gifted and talented.* Ventura, CA : Ventura County Superintended of Schools Office.

Renzulli, Joseph. 1978. What makes giftedness? Re-examining a definition. *Phi Delta Kappan, 60*(3): 180-184, 186.

Rohrer, June. 1995. Primary teacher conceptions of giftedness: Image, evidence, and nonevidence. *Journal for the Education of the Gifted, 18:* 269-283.

Salend, Spencer. 2005. *Creating inclusive classroom: Effective and reflective practices for all students.* Columbus, OH: Merrill and Prentice Hall.

Siegle, Del. 2001. Teacher bias in identifying gifted and talented students. Paper presented at the Council for Exceptional Children Annual Convention, April in Missouri, U.S.A.

'Poor Girls': A Comparative Analysis Of Their Educational Experiences In England And India

Mary Thornton
University of Hertfordshire, UK
Ponni Iyer
Guru Nanak College of Education, India

Introduction

Gender discrimination is prevalent in many societies, but poverty adds greatly to the experience of disadvantage, not least in terms of equality of educational opportunity and outcomes. The term *poor girls* refers to a double disadvantage that some face with regards to gender and socio-economic status, namely, being female and being poor.

This essay presents a comparative analysis of the educational experiences and outcomes for poor girls in two diverse cultures that share a colonial history and important cultural links. We adopt a social-constructivist perspective (Moore 2000, 32) in order to identify the nature and extent of barriers to educational equality, of discrimination and disadvantage for poor girls in these two countries. We will show how their educational experiences are mediated and shaped in relation to, and in interaction with, the social structures and cultural features of the societies in which they are located. In so doing we recognize the ways in which power relations within each society impact on and shape those experiences.

England is an economically well-developed nation epitomizing 'Western Culture'. India represents 'Eastern Culture', with a western colonial influence. It is a developing country with great economic potential and the largest democracy in the world. India goes further than England in terms of equal rights, by permitting positive discrimination in favor of Scheduled Castes, Tribes and Other Backward Castes in the form of reservations and quotas in Government posts and Higher Education (HE). However, India's family and cultural traditions do not encourage individualism or gender equality as much as in the west.

In both countries girls' educational aspirations, opportunities and successes are shaped by the expectations of their significant others, teachers, parents and kinship networks. Income, social class, caste, culture and religion in turn, shape these. The interweaving of these influences is complex, with diverse educational opportunities and outcomes for different groups of girls. However, being female and poor, in India and England is a powerful double-disadvantage.

Poor Girls' Education: An Indian Perspective

"For every woman who sits in Parliament or goes to the Supreme Court to argue a case, you have thousands in the villages who don't even know about their basic rights and that they are equal citizens." (Bumiller 1991, 128)

The girl-child is frequently denied her international right to receive a free education or the opportunity to develop her abilities to become a useful member of society. (Office for the Commission for Human Rights 2007). Indian women have been regarded as the second sex since ancient times. The earliest records identify rules laid down by Manu in 200 B.C.

"By a young girl, by a young woman, or even by an aged one, nothing must be done independently, even in her own house. In childhood a female must be subject to her father, in youth to her husband, when her lord is dead to her sons; a woman must never be independent." (Coonrod 1998, under "India: An Overview" section, para. 9) [an unpaginated electronic work]

Although the Indian constitution grants women equal rights, strong patriarchal traditions persist, with women's lives shaped by customs that are centuries old. There remains today gross differentiation in their access to education and infrastructure facilities, employment opportunities and social support systems compared to men. There are differences between rural and urban women in their standard of living, their cultural beliefs and their practices. There is also disparity of treatment of women among Indian states.

The Poverty Line

According to the United Nations Development Program report 2006, India ranks 127 in The Human Development Index. The percentage of Indians living below the poverty line was twenty-two percent in 2004 to 05. This translates to around eighty million people. According to experts, the official poverty lines of Rs. 368 (US$9 in rural areas) and Rs. 559 (US$14 in urban areas) per person per month are unsatisfactory and should be renamed starvation lines because, apart from factoring 650 grams of food grains daily, they make little provision for the other essentials of life such as shelter, clothing, healthcare, sanitation, drinking water and education (Guruswamy and Abraham 2004). The economic implications of investment in girls' education in India are normally viewed from patriarchal attitudes that render the girl child an economic liability.

Education in India

According to Peiris (citing UNICEF 1999), eighty percent of urban Indian children went to school, but in rural areas the figure was only twenty percent. In Kerala ninety percent went to school, but in Bihar the figure was only fifty percent. According to Pratham Charitable Trust 2006, nearly eleven million children are out of school. The lack of availability of schools in rural India is a serious issue directly affecting access to education, especially for girls (National Commission on Education 2007)

Economic Barriers

The low value placed on girls and women in Indian society contributes to families' decisions not to invest in their daughters' education. For many poorer communities girls are most valued as wage earners. Schooling girls is seen as a double expense — expenditure cost and loss in terms of income. The role of the rural girl at home is starkly different from that of her brothers. She cooks, cleans, tends to younger siblings, and fetches water and wood for daily needs, spending fifteen to thirty percent more time working than boys (USAID India 2005). She is often the last to eat and fed the least. Even in urban environments the education of the girl child carries an economic cost. She will become the property of her husband's family when she marries; a dowry will need to be paid; her labor will benefit her husband's family (not her natal one) and, unlike sons, she bears no responsibility to help maintain her parents in old age. She is therefore an economic liability rather than an asset.

Socio-Cultural Barriers

Despite laws preventing dowry and child marriage these customs persist, perpetuating the incidence of female foeticide, infanticide, and general neglect. Mortality rates for girls aged one to five are fifty percent higher than for boys. As the United Nations Development Program puts it, young lives are lost each year, "because of the disadvantage associated with being born with two X chromosomes" (quoted in Norohna 2006). In 2001 the all-India sex ratio was 927 girls for every thousand boys, putting the country right at the bottom of the global charts, worse off than countries like Nigeria (965) and Pakistan (958), with only China below it (with a ratio of 832 for every thousand boys). Eighty percent of India's districts show a decline in sex ratios since 1991, with Punjab State bottom, counting less than eight hundred per one thousand males (UNICEF 2006). This 'missing girls' syndrome is part of an Indian social dilemma, interwoven with general gender biases.

Educational Barriers

Thakore (2004, para. 10) cites Pant (1995) as suggesting that, "The desire or motivation to send girls to school and ensure its completion is circumscribed by high economic costs, unfriendly school environments and social sanctions". Of 1,231,391 habitations or villages in 2002, only 653,076 had lower elementary schools (to class IV), and only 227,146 contained upper elementary schools (to class VIII) (National Council for Educational Research and Training 2005). According to the 2001 census, "For every hundred girls that enroll in school in rural India, forty will reach class IV, eighteen will reach class VIII, nine will reach class IX, and only one will make it to class XII" (Infochange India 2007, under "The Big Questions", para. 4) [an unpaginated electronic work]. Thus the situation for rural girls is dire, with less than half of those who enroll completing lower elementary education and barely one in a hundred completing higher secondary education.

Gender Barriers to Educational and Social Equity

Wealthy families across India have historically supported gender biases that adversely affect women's access to education, especially HE. However, the plight of poor girls is worse, with poverty frequently denying them access to even elementary education. There has always been a large gap between male and female, and urban and rural, literacy rates in India. In the 1991 census thirty-one percent of rural women and fifty-eight percent of rural men were considered literate compared with sixty-four percent of urban women and eighty-two percent of urban men. In the 2001 census the overall literacy rates were seventy-six percent men, fifty-four percent women, and eighty percent urban, sixty percent rural. The major obstacles to girls' literacy and education in India are economic, cultural and educational.

The lack of schools, coupled with absence of basic amenities such as toilets and electricity, and inadequate teaching and learning materials, are a stark reality in rural India. The non-availability of female teachers in many rural schools, the absence of single-sex schools, the location of many schools more than two kilometers from home, are all serious factors discouraging even progressive minded parents from sending their daughters to schools.

When Indian girls manage to progress to HE their course choices are highly gendered. The majority pursue studies in humanities and business rather than Science or IT-related fields. In engineering they account for only one percent (Academy for Educational Development 2007). Today, even with increased opportunities for education and employment, women are still an oppressed class, and especially so in poor rural areas (Infochange India 2007, under "The Big Questions") [an unpaginated electronic work].

The Girl Child Welfare Bill 2006, enacted by the Indian Parliament, is a major step in focusing attention on this vulnerable population. However, while the Dowry Prohibition Act, Child Marriage Restraint Act and other social evils like sexual harassment of women in work places (National Informatics Centre

Karnataka 2007) represent a multitude of laws and government schemes aimed at the welfare of women in India, their implementation and effect on poor women's lives is marginal. While NGOs and Government bodies at state and national levels have undertaken many initiatives to promote the education of the economically disadvantaged girl child, a great deal remains to be done to ensure that these laws and schemes are implemented effectively.

Poor Girls' Education
The English Perspective

Historically, in England as elsewhere, women were the homemakers and men the hunters, literally the breadwinners. Although both had worked equally hard in manual labor in rural areas, following the Industrial Revolution, men became the undisputed heads of households. Middle and upper class women didn't work outside the home, although spinsters could become governesses and later teachers. Respectable poor women (and girls) were employed as servants or worked in the new industries. If educated at all, poor girls were taught basic literacy and numeracy alongside domestic skills, while wealthier girls were taught cultural refinements and social skills such as needlework, music, art and deportment. It was not until 1918 that women over thirty gained the right to vote, and it was not until 1928 that the voting age for women was lowered to the same age as for men (twenty-one at that time). It took another forty years to achieve the right to equal pay (Equal Pay Act 1970).

In England, as in India, there is also formal, legal provision for equality of educational opportunity for boys and girls. There are no formal barriers to the education of girls, no matter their cultural background, ethnicity, wealth or where they live. State schooling is free and compulsory for all children aged five to sixteen years of age, with legal sanctions if parents fail to ensure that their children receive an education. However, formal legal provision and rights do not ensure educational equity, and there exist some significant differences in terms of dropout and educational attainments. In contrast to India, these tend to be experienced more negatively by boys i.e. women now make up fifty-six percent of students in HE and girls get better overall results in national tests. However, national figures mask in-group differences. When HE figures are disaggregated we see that women are far more likely to study part-time, to accommodate work and family responsibilities, and are over-represented on stereotypically female courses, such as humanities, arts, teaching and health care.

Table 1 illustrates differences between boys and girls of different ethnic origins in England. It demonstrates that at age sixteen girls are doing better than boys, and that children of Indian origin are doing very well indeed, second only to their Chinese origin peers. Black Caribbean children do least well, but, even so, Black Caribbean and Black African girls outperform their male peers by the largest margin, and they outperform boys of Pakistani and Bangladeshi origin as well.

Poor children in England generally do considerably less well than wealthier peers aged sixteen, with just 16.6 percent of boys and 22.3 percent of girls who receive free school meals achieving five or more good passes at GCSE (DfES 2006). Nevertheless, at age sixteen, girls from all ethnic groups across all income levels out perform their male counterparts; the lowest school achievers in England today are poor white boys (Abrams 2007).

More women than men enroll in HE, except for British Bangladeshi and British Pakistani women (Higher Education Statistics Agency 2007). This may be due to cultural differences regarding gendered expectations, some of which parallel those endemic in India, such as dowry, early and arranged marriages, and a devaluing of the girl child. While there is great diversity within South-Asian groups in England, with British Indian women doing particularly well in education, there is also evidence that some families maintain negative gender traditions despite being British-born (Jhutti 1998). It is not until we reach the level of full-time higher research degrees that men outnumber women in HE, and this applies across all ethnicities, with just one exception, that of Black British women of Caribbean origin.

Table 1. General Certificate of Secondary Education (GCSE): 2005/06 outcomes by ethnicity and gender:

Ethnicity		% Achieving 5 A* to C grades	
		Boys	Girls
White	White British	40.2	48.2
	Irish	46.2	53.4
Mixed British	White and Black Caribbean	27.4	37.3
	White and Black African	38.4	47.2
	White and Asian	55.8	62.5
British Asian	Indian	54.0	64.2
	Pakistani	30.4	38.8
	Bangladeshi	35.1	42.1
Black British	Caribbean	22.5	35.7
	African	31.3	43.0
British Chinese		59.2	72.0
All pupils		39.7	48.0

Source: Adapted from Table 8 Department for Education and Science (DfES) 2006.

The Poverty Line

The Equal Opportunities Commission (EOC 2006) defines poverty as income below sixty percent of the median. In 2003 this was less than £320 per week (US$631). In 2003 seventeen percent of households were deemed in poverty, rising to twenty percent for households with children. This translates into

2.6 million children living in poverty in Great Britain in 2003 (National Statistics On-Line 2007).

Divisions between rural and urban areas tend towards the reverse of India's, with rural areas more likely to contain affluent suburbs of commuters, and to be community oriented and comprehensive in terms of the educational opportunities available. In urban environments there are marked differences between affluent and poor areas and the schools children attend.

Education in England

Sex segregation by subject was a key feature of early twentieth century compulsory education in England with girls more likely to be taught 'combined science' alongside needlework and cooking, and boys separate sciences alongside vocationally related subjects. Sex segregation by subject was finally eradicated by the introduction of a National Curriculum in 1988. However, this has been undone by re-introducing subject choice and specialization at age fourteen. Subjects are open to all students, but pupils are increasingly making sex-stereotypical choices.

Class inequalities became a concern of government in the 1960s, when compensatory education was introduced (paralleling Headstart in the USA). Gender concerns came later e.g. when King (1971) demonstrated how working class girls did badly in education, and Delamont (1980, 109) wrote that working class girls "are the most under-privileged group of all".

Gender Barriers to Educational and Social Equity

Gender remains an informal obstacle to educational success for poor girls. Romance, motherhood and early marriage appeals to many girls in lower SES groups, and successful career women with equal pay and shared family responsibilities are rarely found within such groups. As in India, the major obstacles are economic, cultural and educational.

Economic

Women earn less, are more likely to work part-time, and within a narrower range of occupations, typically gender-stereotypical ones with lower pay levels. EOC research in 2001 found girls more likely than boys to undertake domestic chores, including shopping, cleaning, washing and cooking, and to care for siblings or infirm relatives.

Cultural

Despite equality in law the reality is somewhat different. Women remain under-represented in powerful positions in England. Just ten percent of senior judges, thirteen percent of University heads and nineteen percent of Members of Parliament are women (EOC 2007b). Gender stereotyping in subject choice in school, and in the workplace persists. Poor women, and especially women from ethnic minorities, have the lowest employment rates, experience the biggest pay gaps and have an even narrower range of occupational choices (EOC 2007c).

Educational

Children from lower SES groups are much less likely to continue to HE than their middle class peers (Stothart 2006). They are more likely to attend less prestigious universities (Quinn et al. 2005) and to drop out or fail their courses (Thomas, Cooper, and Quinn 2001). In terms of power and culture rather than numbers, Quinn (2003, 97) argues that "Class is still structuring and positioning students and their learning experiences", and that "women remain marginalized" (p.148). Poor students prefer to study in communities in which they feel they will fit in, and they self-select into less prestigious institutions for this reason. Degrees from less prestigious universities produce lower economic returns for the financial investment that HE requires, and the need for poor students to work whilst studying inhibits time available for study and the likelihood of good results. HE is a costly and risky business for the poor, and especially for women.

Despite massive investment in widening participation in HE over the past five years the proportion of working class students has barely changed (from twenty-six to twenty-eight percent, Stothart 2006). It is mainly middle class students who have gained from expanded provision. However, it is the lack of achievement and deteriorating behavior of white working class boys that is the main focus of attention in England today.

Summary and Conclusions

Formal, legal barriers to the education of poor girls in England and India are, in this twenty-first century, largely non-existent. However, in India highly persistent cultural norms and values about the education of girls and the position of women remain strong. In England they exist but are much weaker. While we might say that the social value assigned to the girl child in England is relatively neutral, in India it is frequently negative, and this has a devastating impact on their educational opportunities.

Poverty in both countries inhibits the goal of educational and social equality. The poor lack power to assert their rights to what is legally theirs and remain significantly disadvantaged in terms of educational opportunities. In England poor girls are doing a bit better than their poor brothers but informal gender barriers and social inequalities persist. In India gender barriers and inequalities are pervasive and until women and girls are recognized as of equal value to men and boys there will be none poorer than poor girls in India.

References

Arnot, M., M. David, and G. Weiner. 1999. *Closing the gender gap: Postwareducation and social change.* Cambridge: Polity Press.

Abrams, F. 2007. Rescuing the lost boys. *Times Educational Supplement,* London, January 17, Magazine 14-19.
Academy for Educational Development. 2007. India case study: Women and information technology in India. http://projects.aed.org/techequity/India.htm (accessed May 7, 2007).
Bumiller, E. 1991. *May you be the mother of a hundred sons: A journey among the women of India.* New Delhi India: Penguin Books.
Coonrod, C. S. 1998. *Chronic hunger and the status of women in India: The hunger project.* http://www.thp.org/reports/indiawom.htm (accessed May 7, 2007).
Delamont, S. 1980. *Sex roles and the school.* London: Methuen.
Department for Education and Science. 2006. National Curriculum assessment, GCES and equivalent attainment and post-16 attainment by pupil characteristics in England 2005/06 (Provisional). *National Statistics First Release SFR 46/2006.* November 23 . London: DfES. http://www.dfes.gov.uk/rsgateway/DB/SFR/s000693/index.shtml (accessed May 9, 2007).
Equal Opportunities Commission. 2001. Young people and sex stereotyping data. www.eoc.org.uk/Default.aspx?page=15609 (accessed April 21, 2007).
------ . 2006. *Gender and poverty in Britain.* Working Paper Series No.6. York: Social Policy Unit, University of York.
------. 2007a. Ethnic minority women and men — additional Tables. http://www.eoc.org.uk/default.aspx?page=16090 (accessed May 11, 2007).
------ . 2007b. *Sex and Power: who runs Britain?* Manchester: EOC.
------ . 2007c. *Moving on up? The way forward.* Manchester: EOC.
Guruswamy, M., and R. J. Abraham. 2004. The poverty line is a starvation line. *Infochange Agenda.* http://www.infochangeindia.org/agenda6_04.jsp (accessed May 7, 2007).
Higher Education Statistics Agency On-line Information Service. 2007. *Students and qualifiers data tables.* Table 10b, First year UK domiciled HE students by qualification aim, mode of study, gender and ethnicity 2005/06. http://www.hesa.ac.uk/holisdocs/home.htm (accessed May 1, 2007).
Infochange India. 2007. *Infochange Education,* http://www.infochangeindia.org/EducationIbp.jsp - h2 (accessed May 18, 2007).
Jhutti, J. 1999. Dowry among Sikhs in Britain. In *South Asians and the Dowry Problem,* ed. W. Meski, 179-198. Stoke-on-Trent: Trentham Books.
King, R.A. 1971. Unequal access in education — sex and social class. *Social and Economic Administration* 5 (3): 167-75.
Moore, R. 2000. For Knowledge: Traditionalism, progressivism and progress in education — reconstructing the curriculum debate. *Cambridge Journal of Education* 30 (2): 17-36.
National Commission on Education. 2007. Education: Disadvantaged communities, girls, budget analysis and tracking, in 5 states.

http://www.aspbae.org/Edwatch%20Workshop%20Documents/Proposals/India%20Proposal%20updated%2021%20aug.pdf (accessed May 7, 2007).

National Council for Educational Research and Training. 2005. Seventh all India educational survey. http://ncert.nic.in/sites/Annual%20Report/AnnualReport%20English0506/Chap 12.pdf. (accessed May 7, 2007)

National Informatics Centre Karnataka. 2007. Programmes for women's development. http://www.kar.nic.in/dwcd/womdev.pdf (accessed May 7, 2007).

National Statistics Online. 2007. Social inequalities. http://www.statistics.gov.uk/cci/nugget.asp?id=1005 (accessed April 4, 2007).

Norohna, F. 2006, March 6. The gap between rhetoric and reality. http://altindia.blogspot.com/2006/05/india.gap.between.rhetoric andreality.html (accessed May 7, 2007).

Office for the Commission for Human Rights. Declaration of the rights of the child, 1959. www.unhchr.ch/html/menu3/b/25.htm (accessed May 7, 2007).

Pant, N. 1995. *Status of the girl child and women in India.* India: Vendam Books.

Peiris, V. 1999. UNICEF report cites declining levels of education and literacy world-wide. May 19. World Socialist Web Site. http://www.wsws.org/articles/1999/may1999/illi-m19.shtml (accessed May 7, 2007).

Pratham Charitable Trust. 2006. Annual status of education report 2006 (rural) http://www.pratham.org/aser2006.php (accessed May 7, 2007)

Quinn, J. 2003. *Powerful subjects: Are women taking over the university?* Stoke-on-Trent: Trentham Books.

Quinn, J., L. Thomas, K. Slack, L. Casey, W. Thuxton, and J. Noble.2005. *FromLife crisis to life-long learning: Rethinking working class 'dropout' from highereducation.* London: Joseph Rowntree Foundation.

Stothart, C. 2006. Access drive has failed to bridge class divide. *Times Higher.* London. March 17 p.10.

Thakore, D. 2004. Long and arduous road.India together: news in proportion. *http://www.indiatogether.org/2004/apr/edu-parity.htm (*accessed May 7, 2007).

Thomas, L., M. Cooper, and J. Quinn, eds. 2001. *Access to higher education: The unfinished business.* Stoke-on-Trent: The Institute for Access Studies, Staffordshire University and the European Access Network.

Thomas, L., and J. Quinn.2007. *First generation entry into higher education: An international study.* Berkshire: Society for Research into Higher Education and Open University Press.

United Nations Development Program. 2006. Human development report 2006: Human Development Indicators. http://hdr.undp.org/hdr2006/statistics/countries/country_fact_sheets/cty_fs_IND.html (accessed May 7, 2007).

UNICEF. 2006. State of the world's children report. http://www.unicef.org/sowc06/ (accessed May 7, 2007).
USAID India. 2005. Strategy 2003-2007. Strategic objective 5: Enhanced opportunities for vulnerable people. http://www.usaid.gov/in/our_work/strategy/strategy8.htm (accessed May 7, 2007)

Access to Education: A Distant Dream For Many in India

Gowri Parameswaran
State University of New York at New Paltz, USA

Introduction: Caste in India

Sixteen percent of India's population is composed of individuals belonging to a group alternatively called *depressed classes, scheduled caste, Untouchable, Harijan* or *Dalit* (Government of India 1997). Over the last 100 years, India has seen rising activism and self-consciousness among members of the group and in 1939, the more assertive leaders of the untouchable caste, formally named themselves *Dalit*. Members of the group, about 150 million, (Government of India 2006) today prefer to call themselves *Dalit* or the 'broken people' as a sign of resistance to the Hindu caste ideology. Many prominent historians believe that caste practices are centuries old and are a result of protracted struggles over land and resources between new immigrants and the earlier inhabitants of India (Jaffrelot 2005; Mendelsohn & Vicziany 1998).

Members of the untouchable community were not allowed to follow the traditional Hindu rituals that the upper castes practiced, thus denying them the right to be 'reborn' like the privileged castes (Berreman 1979; Kolenda 1978). Throughout history, *Dalits* were at the bottom of the Indian caste hierarchy, wherein they were denied access to the many amenities that upper caste Hindus enjoyed. They were deprived of access to public drinking water, walking on public roads, and entry into upper-caste places of worship. In some parts of the country, basic human dignities, like women being allowed to cover their upper bodies, were denied to *Dalits* (Jaoul 2006). In some parts of the country even the shadow of a *Dalit* falling on upper-caste individuals was considered polluting and severe punishment was meted out to the person and his or her family who committed the infraction (Raheja 1988; Rao 2007).

Since India's independence in 1947, leaders of mainstream India as well as the leaders of these highly marginalized groups have recognized the severity and longevity of oppressions meted out against members of the untouchable and tribal communities, by upper caste Hindus and the need to ameliorate the dreadful conditions under which they lived (ABACUS 2001; Cunningham 1999; United Nations 1993).

One of the principal architects of the original constitution of India was Dr. Ambedkar who was himself from a schedule caste community. He had overcome steep hurdles to train himself as a lawyer and understood that the moment after independence had to be seized in order to level the playing field of opportunities for the marginalized peoples of India (Jaoul 2006). Dr. Ambedkar enshrined within the constitution several articles that explicitly offer directives aimed at improving the lot of the most disadvantaged populations within India: the Indian constitution makes it a crime to practice untouchability. It also mandates that both states and central government must offer and implement preferential treatment towards correcting past wrongs. (Keer 1990; Kolenda 1978; Sen 2000).

The State of Dalit Access to Education

It cannot be said that the situation with regards to inequality and the force and strength of upper caste oppression over the lower castes has remained the same for marginalized communities in India over the last half a century. Overall, the quota system for *Dalit*s and other oppressed groups has been quite effective in that the percentage of *Dalit*s and tribal community members in government jobs and in institutions of higher learning has more than doubled since 1990. In several regions of the country, there are now major political leaders who hail from these communities and they have implemented policies that are aimed at the advancement of these marginalized communities. However, much of the improved access to jobs and higher education has benefited the better off among these groups while the vast majority of the population still lives in poverty (Berreman 1979; Jaffelot 2005; Jaoul 2006).

In India, an examination of elementary school enrollment indicates that there has clearly been a lowering of gender and class disparities across most of the country. The gross enrollment rate has risen to 98 % by 2005 (Department of Education 2006; UNESCO 2000). Many social scientists have attributed massive enrollment drives, the rising participation of parents and the all-India midday meal scheme for this incredible achievement (Ajwad 2006; UNICEF 2001; UNICEF 2002). A constitutional amendment was passed in 2002 making education a human rights issue in the Indian parliament (Government of India, 2003). However, there have been several barriers to educational equity with regards to *Dalit*s (Mehrotra, Panchamukhi, Srivastava, & Srivastava, 2005; National Sample Survey, 2000; Ramachandran, 2002; 2004). These are listed below:

Physical Location Barriers:

Perhaps one of the major barriers to schooling is the physical location of schools themselves. In India most villages are divided into hamlets, each being typically dominated by a particular caste. When there is only one school allocated for several hamlets, children are reluctant to cross borders into an alien hamlet for fear of invoking caste tensions. Many of the public (government sponsored) schools in India are located at the center of village and rural communities. The spaces here are historically dominated by upper caste Hindus while *Dalit*s and Tribal Community members live at least a kilometer away from the center (Pratham 2006).

Although the laws in India prevent the practice of 'untouchability,' the practice of caste ritual pollution is alive in rural communities. Lower caste and tribal children are prevented from entering village centers either overtly or covertly, by privileged Hindus. Sometimes sheer distance prevents families from allowing their children to walk to schools. Thus government schools become inaccessible for minority children (Probe 1999).

Hostility in Schools

Government schools can provide a very hostile environment in many ways. Lack of teachers from *Dalit* and Tribal backgrounds is a serious problem and the Indian government has offered few incentives for teacher-training institutions to target minority recruits in their institution. Since earning a teaching certificate is only possible after finishing one's baccalaureate degree in India, it is a very expensive proposition for most poor families. Caste considerations play a role in job selection procedures in a field dominated by upper caste Hindus. In some parts of the country, local bureaucrats are paid bribes to procure teaching jobs in a government-run school. Public school teaching is not a respected profession in India today because of the low pay and poor working conditions in government-run schools as opposed to private educational settings (Abacus 2001; Jeffrelot 2005)

Lack of Minority Teachers

Lack of teachers from marginalized religious, caste, economic and regional backgrounds have serious consequences in both enrollment and retaining of children from these backgrounds (UNICEF 2005; UNICEF 2006). The most obvious effect is lack of a role model for achievement for children from disadvantaged backgrounds. There have been a number of studies pointing to the importance of a role model in raising performance levels and self-esteem of children from communities who have historically been denied access to educational opportunities (Visaria & Ramachandran 2003).

Another consequence of a lack of minority teachers and administrators in schools has been that blatant acts of discrimination and prejudice are not challenged within schools. A number of studies have pointed to upper-caste teachers bringing their own caste-based biases about social hierarchy with them

(Ramachandran 2004). One United Nation's report documents that *Dalit*s are often treated like servants in the classroom. They clean classrooms and run errands for teachers and administrators (UN 2006). When a school is located in *Dalit* areas, there are higher levels of teacher absenteeism (Kabeer 2006). In another study conducted across the country, *Dalit* children reported that they were made to sit separately in schools and teachers often refused to touch their slates to check their answers (Abacus, 2006).

Dalit and tribal students report other more subtle forms of discrimination based on values, expectations and attitudes towards them. In a PROBE study (Nambisan 1998), one teacher openly dismissed the value of schooling for the poor. With such persistent occurrences of prejudice that teachers exhibit towards disadvantaged children, a lack of an authority figure to confide in could dissuade children from attending school regularly.

Gender, caste and schooling

Gender has been shown to be a major factor in leveling the playing field in terms of opportunities for children from all backgrounds (Bhattacharya 2003). Reasons that girls find schools inaccessible are numerous. One major factor is lack of female teachers from their own backgrounds. In rural communities families are much less likely to send their daughter to school if they fear communal recriminations. These recriminations result in an inability to find an appropriate groom for the daughter as men assume that educated wives are more likely to challenge them (Visaria & Ramachandran 2003). Rural schools are in extreme states of disrepair making girls' bathrooms unusable or lacking privacy; thus families of girls perceive schools as being dangerous spaces (Patnaik & Dingwaney 1985). Often daughters may be enlisted to take care of aging grandparents and/or other siblings while parents are away at work. They might thus be unavailable to attend school during the day when most government run schools operate (Jha & Dhir 2005).

Curriculum Issues

The standard curriculum followed by the centralized school systems in India is ill-equipped to deal with the specific needs of children from lower caste and tribal communities that have been historically oppressed. In the average curriculum across the country there are few references made to the enormous power that caste affiliations have wielded both in the past and continue to wield into present-day politics. One study of textbooks in the state of Madhya-Pradesh indicated that there was not one reference to a *Dalit* character in any context, even though a large number of students in these schools come from untouchable communities (ABACUS 2001). It is not until one's post-graduate education, that a student is forced to seriously engage with caste as a political, economic, and social force. This kind of serious engagement with caste oppression and upper caste privilege as a topic of study is available only if a student chooses to concentrate on the social sciences. Therefore the vast majority of the Indian public is uninformed about the caste system and its impact on India's history (Deshpande 2006)).

Dalit researchers have pointed out that caste, as is defined today, has basically been a colonial creation, to aid in administration matters and for helping to classify the so-called 'criminal castes.' Much of the description of India's history has been from a mainstream perspective whether it involved the various dynasties that ruled India prior to the coming of the Europeans, or when describing the freedom struggle. The resources that have been used to bolster historical arguments have been mainly from Sanskrit, the language of the elite in India (Pratham 2006; Probe 1999). *Dalit* researchers point to the importance of bringing in voices from the margins and including written and oral histories in languages that were not spoken by the privileged castes (Jaoul 2006).

Paving the Path to Equity

There are several major barriers to equity and access in education that have to be addressed by the government of India and policy makers in order to open up education for all. These are:

Lack of Government Investment in Public Education

The government of India has invested very little in the education of the marginalized. The government invests a mere 3% of its annual budget on education and a fraction of this amount is allocated to primary education (Jha & Dhir 2005). Thus even though there are quotas in place to secure seats for *Dalit* applicants, not many students from the lower castes are able to pass the numerous gate-keeping exams to get there (Deshpande 2006). In fact, it is the wealthier among the marginalized castes that are able to send their children to private schools where the quality of education enables them to qualify for higher-education institutions. This problem is especially acute in professional institutions that lead to better-paying occupations like engineering and medicine. It is imperative that the government invest more in primary and secondary public schooling, making sure that students have decent school buildings, safe teaching environments and access to books to learn (ABACUS 2001; Kabeer 2006; Mehrotra 2006; UNICEF 2002).

Addressing Girls' Education

The discrepancy between the educational attainment of girls as compared to boys in *Dalit* communities far outstrips gender differences in educational achievement among the upper castes. Public schooling needs to be made flexible in order to surmount the hurdles that *Dalit* girls undergo in order to complete basic schooling. School administrators must ensure safety within schools by increased monitoring of the physical spaces within which sexual harassment tends to occur. Even though *Dalit*s in general are rarely mentioned in textbooks, *Dalit* women are even more invisible in the recounting of Indian history (Berreman 1979). There is clearly documented evidence of the many women leaders from the community who had fought against the British during the height of the freedom struggle. *Dalit* Women leaders like Ruth Manorama and Mayawati are forcing Indian society to rethink both caste and gender as defining identities for people. The school curriculum needs to reflect these changes in power in Indian politics and society.

Introducing Compulsory Dalit Studies

In the mid-1980s scholars who were interested in issues of social justice and marginalization in India proposed a '*Dalit* Studies' curriculum similar to 'women's studies' and 'black studies' in Western institutions. There has been no serious engagement by Indian academic institutions with the historical injustices perpetrated by the Indian caste system and the current forms of hegemony this hierarchy has taken. The project has yet to take a concrete national shape with coherent critical theory and understandings of the experiences of *Dalit*s.

The teaching of *Dalit* literature and history at all levels of school education is imperative. Much of the literature in regional languages taught in schools is written by upper caste Hindus who do not have any understanding of *Dalit* life. Whether in literature or in the social sciences in schools, lower caste members are invisible. Even when *Dalit* life is portrayed it is often from the perspective of an upper caste writer. It is important to provide a realistic view of *Dalit* life in contemporary India (Limbale 2004).

Education for Equity

It is important for the educational policies of the Indian government to be inclusive of all dialects, especially those that pertain to the most marginalized of communities. There is lack of reading materials incorporated in the official curriculum that includes the dialects of *Dalit*s. There are internationally funded NGOs that are engaged in developing curriculum materials aimed at engaging minority students in their native languages and dialects. There has to be better connections established with these organizations so that public schools can also benefit from the availability of these materials (Sharma 1999).

Incorporating *Dalit* music in the school curriculum is very important. Indian schools have a very meager curriculum in the arts. When music or painting is taught, high caste and upper class traditions tend to dominate art activities in schools. However, *Dalit*s have been expressing their outrage at the oppression and injustice that they have faced throughout centuries through music and art. Many *Dalit* community members had been hired as drummers and mourners at funerals and weddings through the centuries and there is a strong musical tradition among them. Most songs involved mourning over loss, singing about heroes who challenged caste hierarchy and were murdered as a result of their protests, lullabies and community celebration songs. These have been passed down from one generation to the other orally and still form the living culture of oppressed communities. There has been a resurgence of various forms of street theater among communities that occupy the lowest rungs of Hindu society and these have yet to make their way into schools. Thus *Dalit* history, culture and traditions have not been used very effectively towards promoting universal literacy in public schooling (Limbale 2004).

A Successful Model

Kerala is a state in the south of India and forms the very tip of the Indian subcontinent. It has a population of 32 million people. Historically, it has had one of the most rigid of social systems based on caste where people of the lowest section of the caste hierarchy were often physically punished and even put to death for the slightest of infractions. In the last century, it has transformed itself from one of the most socially unequal state in India to one of the most progressive in terms of its social policies. It was one of the first states where untouchables agitated to throw out caste pollution rituals.

With the drafting of the Kochi declaration in 1990, Kerala decided to take practical steps to ensure that primary and secondary education is available for all its citizens, especially those from the most marginalized segments of its society. It called for the Indian government to make the right to education a question of human rights thus emphasizing its importance in terms of policy initiatives and resources allotted to it. The state spends close to 47 % of its income on education, which is the highest in India. In 1947, the percentage of Keralites who were literate was 25 %; today it is close to 95 %, which is the highest in India (Mukundan & Bray 2004). In 1992, the newly introduced Kerala Municipal act promised people more participation at local governance in all areas of public life including education.

Leaders at the local level realized the importance of women and girls' participation for the educational programs to be successful. Since many of the women and girls had to perform manual labor besides coming home and doing household chores, mobile libraries were set up that brought books to women in areas where books were not available. In order to enable knowledge of science to revolutionize peoples' lives, rural science fora were held in many areas in the state to discuss and conceive of ways to create a sustainable society. All these activities have transformed marginalized communities across Kerala in a significant manner. Tribal and *Dalit* communities have recently launched several legal challenges against corporations that have attempted to use public resources in unsustainable ways. The increased social and political consciousness of disenfranchised communities in Kerala is a direct result of the progress made on the educational front. Thus, though there are problems with Kerala's education and employment programs, they offer a strong model for other states to try decentralization and equity as guiding principles for their own development programs.

Conclusion

In spite of the numerous issues confronting development in general and education in particular in India, majority of children from the 'untouchable' community are not sent to primary school because of the economic position of *Dalit* families. Many of them rely on their children to bring in financial resources needed to keep from starving. Unless the Indian government takes concerted measures to deal with this larger issue of inequality in wealth and income distribution, all the other steps become mere band-aids that attempt to heal a deep wound (Ajwad 2006; de Haan 2005).

References

ABACUS. 27. *Annual report and plan of action for 2002* [electronic]. Ashanet 2001[cited 27]. Available from http://www.ashanet.org/projects-new/documents/27/annual-report-2001.htm.
———. 2008. Evaluation Studies 2006 [cited October 2 2008]. Available from http://avehiabacus.org/evaluation.html
Ajwad, Mohamed, 2006. *Anti-poverty programs in Uttar Pradesh*. Washington, DC: World Bank Pub.
Berreman, Gerald. 1979. *Caste and Other Inequities: Essays on Inequality*. New Delhi, India: Manohar Book Service.
Bhattacharya, Sabyasachi. *Educating the nation: Documents on the discourse of national education*. New Delhi, India: Vedam Books.
Cunningham, Clark. 1999. *Affirmative Action: India's Example*. Civil Right Journal 12:22-27.
de Haan, Arjan. 2005. Social Policy: Towards Inclusive Institutions. In World Bank Conference '*New Frontiers of Social Policy: Development in a Globalizing World*'. University of Guelph and Department for International Development, UK.
Deshpande, Satish. 2006. *Affirmative action in India and the USA: Equity and Development.*New Delhi: Sage Publication.
Education, Department of. 2006. *Sarva Shiksha Abhiyan: Fourth joint Review* New Delhi: NCERT.
Franke, Richard. 2007. Kerala State, India: radical reform as development. *Monthly Review* 13:24-32.
Gupta, Sneh. 1996. "Recent economic reforms in India and their impact on the poor and vulnerable sections of society." In *Economic reforms and poverty alleviation in India*, edited by H. H. R. and. H. Linneman. New Delhi: Sage.
India, Government of. 2002. *Selected Educational Statistics*. New Delhi: India

Department of Education.
———. 2003. *Tenth Five-Year Plan 2003-2007*. New Delhi: Planning Commission.
Jaffrelot,Christophe. 2005. *Dr. Ambedkar and Untouchability: Analyzing and Fighting Caste*. New Delhi: Sage.
Jaoul, Nicholas. 2006. Learning the use of symbolic means: *Dalit*s, Ambedkar statues and the state of UP. *Contributions to Indian Sociology* 40 (2):175-207.
Jha, Jyotsna. & Dhir, Jingran. 2005. *Elementary Education for the Poorest and Other Deprived Groups*. New Delhi: Manohar Publishers.
Jordan, Beth. 1996. *A theory of poverty and exclusion*. Cambridge, MA: Blackwell Publishers Inc.
Kabeer, Naila. 2006. Social Exclusion and the MDGs: the challenge of durable inequalities in the Asian context. In *Asia 2015 Conference,* January 20-24. Chennai, India.
Keer, Dhananjay. 1990. *Dr. Ambedkar: Life and Mission*. Bombay: Popular Prakashan.
Kolenda, Pauline. M. 1978. *Caste in contemporary India: Beyond organic solidarity*. Prospect Heights, IL: Waveland Press
Limbale, Sudhir. 2004. *Towards an aesthetic of Dalit literature*. New Delhi, India: Orient Longman.
Mandelbaum, David. 1970. Society in India. Los Angeles: University of California Press.
Mehrotra, Santosh. 2006. *Caste and Human Development in India: Explaining a North-South Divide*. New Delhi, India: Sage Publications Inc.
Mehrotra, Santosh & Panchamukhi, Purnima. & Srivastava, Ranjana. and Srivastava, Ravi. 2005. *Universalizing Elementary Education in India: Uncaging the 'Tiger Economy,'*. New Delhi: Oxford University Press.
Mendelsohn, Oliver & Vicziany, Marika. 1998. *The Untouchables, Subordination, Poverty and the State in Modern India*. Cambridge, UK: Cambridge University Press.
Mukundan, Mullikottu-Veettil. & Bray, M.ark 2004. The Decentralisation Of Education In Kerala State, India: Rhetoric And Reality. *Review of Education* 50 (3):22-244.
PRATHAM. 2006. *Annual Status of Education Report*. New Delhi: Pratham Trust.
PROBE. 1999. *India Education Report*. New Delhi: (NCERT).
Ramachandran, Vimala. 2002. *Gender and Social Equity in Primary Education*. New Delhi: European Commission.
———. 2004. *Gender and Social Equity in Primary Education: Hierarchies of Access*. New Delhi: Sage Publications Inc.
Rao, Y. C. 2007. *Writing Dalit History and Other Essays*. New Delhi: India Kanishka Publishers.
Research, MODE. 1995. *Attitudes Study on Elementary Education in India — A Consolidated Report*. New Delhi, India: NCERT.

Sen, Amartya. 2000. *Social Exclusion: Concept, Application and Scrutiny*, Office of Environment and Social Development. Manila, Phillipines: Asia Development Bank.

Shah, Ghanshyam, Harsh Mandar.; Thorat, S.; Deshpande Sudhir.; and Baviskar, Amita. 2006. *Untouchability in rural India*. New Delhi: Sage Publications India Pvt. Ltd.

Sharma, B. K. 1998. *The origin of caste system in Hinduism and its relevance in the present context*. Kathmandu, Nepal: Samdan Publishers.

Sheth, D. L. 2004. *Caste, Ethnicity and Exclusion in South Asia: The Role of Affirmative Action Policies in Building Inclusive Societies*. Islamabad: UNHRD.

UN. 1993. *World Summit for Social Development: The Copenhagen Declaration and Programme of Action*. New York: United Nations.

———. 2006. *The State of the World's Children Report: Excluded and Invisible*. New York: Institution.

UNICEF. 2000. *All India Educataion Report*, edited by UNICEF. New Delhi: Department of Women and Child Development

———. 2002. *Multiple Indicator Survey: India Summary Report*, edited by UNICEF. New Delhi: Department of Women and Child Development.

———. 2005. *The state of the world's children: a report: childhood under threat*. New York, NY: UNICEF.

Visaria, Leela and Ramachandran, Vimala. 2003. What DPEP and other data sources reveal. In *Gender and Social Equity in Primary Education: Hierarchies of Access*, edited by V. Ramachandran. New Delhi: Sage Publications.

Zachariah, Matthew 2006. *Local Democracy and Development: the Kerala People's Campaign for Decentralized Planning*. Journal of Third World Studies 23 (2):45-59.

Social Justice Issues in Higher Education

Social Justice And Higher Education For All: The Bolivarian University of Venezuela

Thomas Muhr
University of Bristol, England

Introduction

By the late 1990s, Venezuela's polyarchic regime that had ruled the country since 1958 had entered a crisis of hegemony which culminated in Hugo Rafael Chávez Frías' election as president in 1998. From the outset, the "Bolivarian Revolution" has been a counter-hegemonic globalisation project driven and legitimated by the democratic concerns of social justice, equity and equality. At the time of Chávez' first election, income-based poverty in Venezuela had increased from 33% in 1975 to 67%, and the middle class had shrunk from 57% to 31%. Income distribution had deteriorated to the 1970 level, when the poorest fifth of Venezuelans received 3% of income, as compared to 53-54% of the richest quintile. Educational segregation mirrored the dramatic social inequality: while Venezuela's wealthy sectors could substantially increase their higher education (HE) participation from the early 1980s on, the poorer half saw their access significantly diminishing. This trend had been reinforced by neoliberal 'Washington Consensus'-driven education 'decentralisation' between 1989 and 1998, which contributed to educational exclusion of the poor from grade 7 on.[1]

Based on 13 months of ESRC-funded critical ethnographic PhD fieldwork in Venezuela (2005-2007), this essay analyses policies and practices of democracy and social justice with respect to the government's higher education for all (HEFA) strategy and the role of the Bolivarian University of Venezuela (UBV) therein. I draw on the Constitution of the Bolivarian Republic of Venezuela (CBRV), national development plans, interviews with officials, coordinators, academics and practitioners, and reflexive active participation in UBV and a deprived urban community in Coro, North-Western Venezuela.

Rights and Democracy

The Preamble of the 1999 CBRV provides the normative base for "refounding" the Republic as a participatory and protagonistic democracy, where the right to social justice implies a challenge to the hegemonic poverty reduction discourses and their disregard of egalitarian principles of distributive justice (cf Pogge 2007). By integrating the major international human rights treaties and covenants, CBRV widens the liberal (civil-political) rights agenda to incorporate comprehensive individual and collective social, economic and cultural rights to the benefit of Venezuela's historically discriminated majority (the poor, women, indigenous peoples, etc.). In education, the constitutional framework transcends the international normative agreements and instruments: Articles 102/103 define "permanent integral quality education" as a human right, an essential root of democracy, and a "public service". Education is geared towards the full development of the person in a democratic society and towards "active, conscious and solidarian participation" in the transformatory processes. To enhance equity, education has been made compulsory from the nursery to the medium diversified level (age 18), and *free* state-provided education includes the undergraduate HE/university level. "Equal conditions and opportunities" for all, with explicit reference to people with a disability, special needs, and inmates, refers to no access restrictions other than those derived from ability, vocation and aspiration (Article 103).

Structurally supported by a significant expansion of access to education at *all* levels, the government's HEFA strategy assumes a pivotal role in the country's "endogenous sustainable development" and the transition towards a "21st - Century Socialism". In order to repay the historically accumulated social debt, the share of the social budget of overall GDP has been raised from 8.2% in 1998 to 13.8% in 2006[2] while, as can be calculated from the Finance Ministry's yearly report, 15.5% of total government spending went to the education sector (MF, 2007: 366). Since 2003, the formal social system has been complemented by over 20 socio-cultural and economic-political 'missions' (*misiones*) that combine immediate poverty alleviation with long-term structural transformation.

CBRV further establishes the philosophical cornerstones of "revolutionary democracy", which combines representative, participatory and direct democracy. While 'participatory democracy' emphasizes people's social, political, economic, and cultural human rights-based protagonism primarily facilitated by the missions, 'direct democracy' refers to Marx' popular control of the means of production and organization in councils. As Table 1 shows, revolutionary democracy expands the functional dimension of public power from the traditional powers (judiciary, legislative, executive) by "electoral power" (the National

Electoral Council) and "citizen power" (Ombuds/wo/man, Comptroller General, and the Public Prosecutor).

Of greater significance to the purposes of this essay, however, is the expansion of the territorial distribution of power by "popular power". Independent of suffrage and elections, popular power is exercised by the organised society through, for instance, community, workers' and student councils. By embodying an inclusive concept of citizenship, popular power can — and should — be exercised by "everybody" residing in the national territory independent of nationality (Article 132, CBRV).

Table 1: Bolivarian distribution of power

PUBLIC POWER	
Territorial Distribution	Functional Distribution
• **Popular Power** • Municipal Power • [Federal] State Power • National Power	• Legislative Power • Executive Power • Judicial Power • **Citizen Power** • **Electoral Power**

Justice and Opportunities

CBRV's ethical-normative framework is translated into policy by the 2001 and 2007 National Development Plans (RBV 2001; 2007). As with the concept of revolutionary democracy, Bolivarian social justice attempts to reconcile socialist with liberal philosophy, i.e. productive, appropriative and distributive justice, which George DeMartino (2003) subsumes as "class justice", and 'bourgeois' rights, to which Mehmet Tabak (2003) refers as "political justice". I look into meanings and implications of the two concepts, before turning to the principle of universality.

Class Justice

In his *Critique of the Gotha Programme*, Marx establishes two principles of justice: one for the *lower*, socialist phase of communist society, i.e. the transition from capitalism to communism, where "the individual producer receives back from society — after the deductions have been made — exactly what he gives to it". For the *higher* phase of communism, he devises "from each according to his ability, to each according to his needs" (Marx 1942, 563-66). The two normative principles bear three co-existing, non-hierarchical moments of class justice: 'productive justice' (*from each*), which refers to the allocation of the labour required for social surplus production; 'appropriative justice', which is the fairness by which individuals or sectors of the society appropriate the surplus produced by others or by themselves; and 'distributive justice' (*to each*), the distribution of the share of the social surplus destined for consumption (DeMartino 2003).

The 2007 Development Plan, which directly refers to the three elements as "new forms of generation, appropriation and distribution of the economic surplus" within a "socialist model of production", applies Marx' *socialist* principle to the social production enterprises, which form the economic core of 21st Century Socialism. Their "resultant economic surplus" is to be appropriated by the workers, and "divided up in proportion to the amount of contributed work" (RBV 2007, 24-25). Marx' primary concern, however, was not distribution, but appropriation, which is determined by the mode and ownership of the means of production: "A radical change in the mode of production would automatically bring about a similar alteration in distribution" (McBride 1975, 206). Therefore, public control of the means of production would be "the first condition of a just post-capitalist society" (Schedler 1978, 227).

Political Justice

Although Marx (1942, 564) viewed the socialist distributive principle of justice necessary in the transition to communism, to him it also exemplified the unjust nature of bourgeois right, whose principle of equality disregards differences between individuals (strength, intelligence, number of dependents etc.). Starkly contrasting Marx' contempt for liberal rights, Venezuela fuses the communist principle "giving to each according to their needs" (RBV 2001, 92) with CBRV's commitment to all 'generations' of human rights to achieve "greatest social happiness" (RBV 2007, 8-9; 12-13).

In Venezuela today, Marx' (1942, 567) demand for justice, i.e. "cooperative property", materializes in the effort of transforming the historical oil rent dependency into a productive social-popular, humanist economy. In this effort, the government reclaims the original idea of "sustainable development" (SD) prior to its cooptation by the mainstream development community into a 'greening of the status quo' (at best) or 'sustained economic growth' (at worst). The Bolivarian idea of the "democratic socialist society" resynthesizes SD's original precepts of intergenerational responsibility, environmental sustainability, social equity, and its construction through popular action (see: Lélé 1991; O'Riordan 1993; MCT 2005). While Venezuela is a long way from achieving this ambitious objective, a potential danger is looming: the 'higher phase' distributive principle is anchored in Marx' conviction of future material abundance through unrestricted industrial progress, which is inseparable from accelerated resource use and consumerism. Abundance, then, "was not only a sufficient but also a necessary condition of equality" (Cohen 2000, 114). Today, such "materialist optimism" is unsustainable against the reality of ecological collapse, which is why Cohen (ibid.) argues that the persisting scarcity *requires* demanding equality — impossible without a solid legality (rights). However, Venezuela's current policies and practices resemble more a 'growth with equity' strategy rather than a real redistribution from top to bottom. If the Bolivarian government implicitly presumes an evolution towards a 'higher phase' of communism — as could be surmised considering the recurring, not to say notorious, celebration of successive economic growth — then the social equity policies would be caught in an irreconcilable contradiction with sustainable development.

Universality

According to Barry (2005, 41; italics original), truly 'equal opportunities' are provided if the "net results of *all* economically relevant factors beyond people's control" are equalised. Venezuela strives for this ideal through its system of missions. As a form of social income, and contrary to assistentialist, focalised welfare programmes, all inhabitants of the national territory are entitled to enjoy the provided social utilities free of charge (RBV 2001, 91/92). They contribute to socio-territorial equality and combine short-term poverty relief with structural change through participation and education (MED 2004). In 2008, 24 missions operate in the areas relevant to endogenous sustainable and human development. In addition to food (*Misión Alimentación*) and free health care (missions *Barrio Adentro I, II, III* and *Milagro*), some of the less referenced examples are: free dental treatment in *Misión Sonrisa*, where functional *and* aesthetic-psychological damages are mended, so that — as the name implies — "the poor can smile again"; while *Misión Negra Hipólita's* mobile care centres provide integral support to the most excluded (street people, HIV/AIDS patients etc.), women's and indigenous people's rights are translated as *Misión Madres del Barrio* (Mothers of the Neighbourhood), which counters the 'feminisation of poverty' in its various dimensions, and *Misión Guiacaipuro* for "ethno-development"; and, in 2006, environmental missions *Arbol* (reforestation) and *Revolución Energética* (free energy-saving light bulbs) were launched. *Milagro* and *Revolución Energética* also operate internationally, for instance to alleviate Nicaragua's prolonged energy crisis. Elementary, fundamental and work-related education and training are provided by Missions *Robinson I, II, III, Ribas*, and *Che Guevara*.

In 2005, as the second country in the hemisphere after Cuba, Venezuela was declared illiteracy-free in accordance with UNESCO standards, and extreme individual poverty was reduced from 20.6% in 1998 to 9.4% in 2007 (RBV, 2008a). The same year, 15.3 million Venezuelans — approximately 55% of the total population — participated in compulsory or non-formal public education, 1.8 million of which enrolled in public HE.[3] While Figure 1 displays the immense increase in gross enrolment at different education levels under the Chávez administration, Figure 2 draws attention to the improved access to HE of Venezuela's poor strata (especially Quintile 1), nevertheless demonstrating the persistent, stark inter-class inequalities.

In sum, Venezuela's concept of "social equity" means a holistic approach to citizenship construction, in which the social, political, cultural and economic dimensions join to transform the structural root causes of injustice and poverty. Key orientations for progressive social inclusion are: universal and equitable enjoyment of the social rights; a reduction of wealth, income and quality of life disparities; and strengthened social participation to generate citizen and popular power (RBV 2001, 91).

The principal mechanism for reconstituting 'the public' as the locus of public power are the Community Councils. They are local instances that integrate a

Community Bank, which facilitates "self-government" through the communities' own development plan. The Banks receive their funding directly from the executive in order to circumvent corruption and political sabotage at the various sub-national levels. Therefore, in addition to the participatory budgeting function, the organised communities are expected to exercise upwards social control over public office holders — including the president. The 2006 Community Councils Law was conceived, and revised in 2007, with active community participation, through a direct democracy mechanism termed Social Street Parliamentarism. The councils increasingly assume a productive-entrepreneurial role in the construction of the "community state".

Figure 1

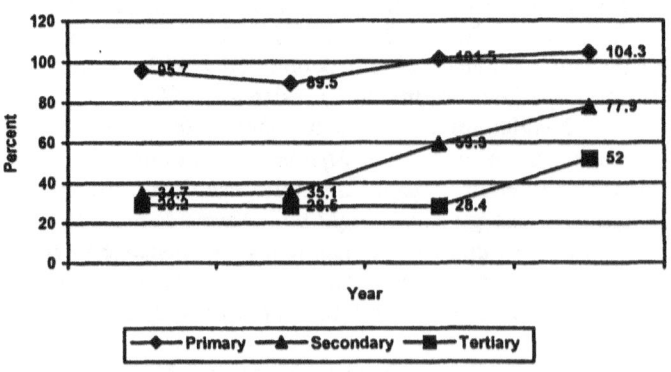

Source: Produced from World Bank data[4]

Figure 2

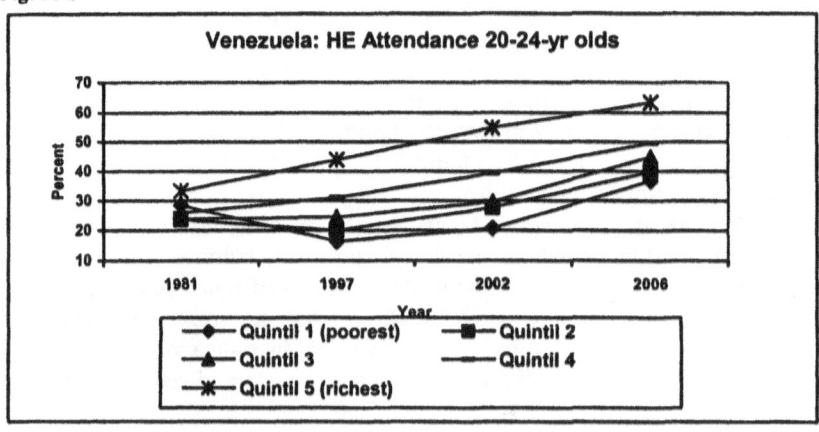

Source: Produced from CEPAL (2008) data.

HEFA: The Municipalized UBV

HE *for all* means that any *bachiller*[5] who *wants* to enter and/or continue tertiary level studies is entitled and actively supported to doing so. Rather than promoting individual social mobility, as was the case with European post-second world war liberal-democratic massification, the objective of HEFA is collective empowerment for 21st Century Socialism. The principal institution in charge of the ambitious objective of universal HE is the Ministry of Higher Education (MES) which, since its creation in 2003, has seen its budget increase 3.6 times, now making up 7.3% of the total national budget, as compared with 6.2% for security and defence (MF 2007, 364; 366).[6]

Equity-enhancing mechanisms comprise free public student transport and targeted studentships: in 2006, almost 240.000 studentships of between US$80-100 each (per month) were awarded to low-income students, which signifies a 339% increase to 2005; over 2500 student loans were converted into grants, and over 23.000 loan debtors had their debts cancelled (MES 2007, 10). Academically, the 'Initial Semester' supports students in revising key knowledge prior to starting their actual studies. In addition, MES has created centres of technical support for students with a visual disability and organizes workshops for the sensibilization of ministry and university staff towards disability (MES 2007). UBV's 12 study programmes are nationally standardized and in part also accommodated in other state-funded universities that have joined the Bolivarian initiative. The initial emphasis on socio-political programmes has gradually been broadened to introduce technical subjects (e.g. Agroecology, Energy Sciences) at the under- and postgraduate levels. Six UBV programmes were municipalized by 2007: Social Communication, Legal Studies, Environmental Management, Social Management of Local Development, Teacher Education, and Integral Community Medicine (ibid., 398). As MES (2007, 400-1) readily concedes, in the municipalities such rapid expansion is naturally accompanied by temporary obstacles and limitations, such as shortages of adequate facilities (libraries, laboratories, computer rooms) and qualified, experienced teaching personnel.

Nevertheless, in order to transform the historical geographies of inequality, *municipalization* is a "quality with equity" strategy (UBV 2004, 95) that combines the immersion of HE in concrete contextual geographies (geo-spatial, geo-historical, geo-social, geo-cultural, geo-economic) with a counter-hegemonic notion of 'quality'. As regards socio-territorial equity, about 2000 *aldeas universitarias* ('university villages', i.e. integral and permanent municipal education spaces) were established in educational institutions, prisons, military garrisons, and libraries in the 335 municipalities by 2007. Increasingly, newly constructed well-equipped standardized *aldeas* aim to ensure "equality in conditions" (UBV 2004, 96). "Deconcentrated decentralisation" means, with respect to UBV, an *aldeas*—regional headquarters—MES satellite structure. Almost 91% of UBV's 158.000 students in 2006 participated in the municipalized *aldeas* (MES 2007, 397). With respect to 'quality', the positivistic notion of quantifiable standards is complemented by "political quality", which refers to the "social relevance" of HE, above all with respect to the construction of citizenship and the exercise of popular power (RBV 2001, 93). Here, two elements should be considered: firstly, the transdisciplinary nature of the study programmes reflects an integral education rationale, as technical education and training joins with ethical-political education. Secondly, the programmes revolve around student-community projects, in which UBV's "social responsibility" in the construction of endogenous development from the local to the national and regional scales is rooted (UBV 2004, 116).

The student-community project fuses theory — a 2 hours/week 'research methods' class — with formative research and prolonged social insertion for knowledge construction in the communities (UBV 2004, 77). As a form of participatory action research (PAR), the research is philosophically guided by people's conscientisation and empowerment in order to become subjects in, and transformers of, their own as well as their community's (and nation's) reality, as theorized in Paulo Freire's action-reflection-action cycle and Jürgen Habermas' emancipatory knowledge. The project groups are interdisciplinary, i.e. formed according to students' geographical origin rather than their respective programmes of study and, as a practice of participatory democracy, the popular sectors determine the research agenda in support of the formation and operation of the Community Councils.

Popular Power in the Community

Rather than a conclusive summary, in this final section I present case study experiences from a marginalized community in Coro (Falcón state), where the various dimensions of HEFA, social equity and democracy converge. To reiterate, Bolivarian holistic development and education counters the traditional notion of education as an isolated variable that would function independent of the unequal and inequitable social structures within which it is embedded (Casanova 2005). From this sociological angle, achieving social equity starts in the street and the home, rather than in the school and the classroom (Albornoz 1999, 172).

Between March-September 2006, and again in July 2007, I accessed the community as a participant in a municipalised UBV PAR group. By March 2006, the group had conducted a community survey and was entering a process of interaction with the community's 'natural leaders', such as members of the Land, Water, or Health Committees, but also shop owners etc. The key actors assumed the role of intermediaries between the students and the community, to mobilize the community for a PAR day (*Diagnóstico Participativo Comunitario*) scheduled for 12th August 2006. Over the weeks, several community meetings were convened to elaborate the research day agenda, either with UBV involvement or autonomously by the community leaders — not always with encouraging results. On one occasion, only six community leaders attended, out of 33 who had originally committed themselves. On the weekend preceding the

PAR day, I joined the UBV students and community leaders going from house to house to inform and motivate the community to participate. To increase the project's viability and legitimacy, they explicitly pointed to the inclusive nature of their community work — as *by* the community *for* the community — rather than for partisan ends.

Between 60-70 community members of all ages participated in the PAR day — a number that the activists considered a success. First, a participatory ranking exercise established a hierarchy of perceived community problems, which subsequently were discussed in working groups (about 4 hours) organized around different topical areas (health, security, land, education, culture, sports, etc.), followed by a plenary session where individual group results were presented. Two days later, the PAR day produced immediate action: as an act of solidarity with the teenagers who had raised the need for a cultural space, the "third age club" felt the social obligation to appropriate an unused building to re-establish a cultural centre. The elder community members remembered that in the past a cultural centre had existed in the community, which, however, at some point was turned into a clinic. Within 1-2 weeks after the occupation, the community had raised funds to renovate the squatted building, moved the clinic there, and reconverted the thus freed space into its original cultural use, which in the course of the following months included establishing a community museum. Crucial for the successful expropriation in the collective interest — as legally facilitated by the CBRV (similar to the European squatter laws prior to the radicalization of neoliberalism in the 1990s) — was the UBV law students' support, which ensured the community's full compliance with the legal requirements, such as formulating an occupation declaration, which was signed by 98 community members, and informing the local police station about the action taken. The fact that the squatted building was owned by a children's foundation (reportedly) presided by the governor's wife — which probably avoided a court case — does not reduce the value of the stated example; namely, UBV's potential to contribute to the generation of popular power and the exercise of academic and popular, 'active social' citizenship.

In this respect, Marx' dismissal of rights on grounds of their bourgeois origin requires reconsideration, as the Bolivarian experience suggests that state law *can* be emancipatory (cf Santos 2002). After all, as Tabak (2003, 536) argues, many of Marx's emancipatory proposals ('freedom' in Marx' terms) today equate with human rights. Nevertheless, my 'smooth' presentation of the revolutionary practices should not suggest that they are free from contradictions, individual power abuses and discrimination. But this is exactly what popular power is designed for to counter, which hinges on a successful reversal of the prevailing apathy created by decades, or centuries, of oppression and dependency. However, despite the perceived "culture of non-participation", as an interviewed lawyer termed the phenomenon, approximately 20.000 councils registered within the first year after the ratification of the Community Councils Law.

References

Albornoz, Orlando. 1999. *Del fraude a la estafa. La educación en Venezuela*. Caracas: UCV.
Barry, Brian. 2005. *Why social justice matters*. Cambridge: Polity.
Casanova, Ramón. 2005. Venezuela después del liberalismo: De los consensos de la reforma de los años noventa a un nuevo contrato educativo? In *Venezuela Visión Plural* (Vol. 1), ed CENDES, 209-41. Caracas: CENDES-UCV.
CEPAL. 2008. *Social indicators and statistics (BADEINSO)*. http://websie.eclac.cl/sisgen/ConsultaIntegrada.asp (accessed May 20, 2008).
Cohen, Gerald A. 2000. *If you're an egalitarian, how come you're so rich?* Cambridge, MA: Harvard University Press.
DeMartino, George. 2003. Realizing class justice. *Rethinking Marxism* 15 (1): 1-31.
Lélé, Sharachchandra M. 1991. Sustainable development: A critical review. *World Development* 19 (6): 607-21.
Marx, Karl. 1942. *Selected works*, Vol 2. London: Lawrence & Wishart.
McBride, William L. 1975. The concept of justice in Marx, Engels, and others. *Ethics* 85 (3): 204-18.
MCT [Ministerio de Ciencia y Technología]. 2005. *Plan nacional de ciencia, tecnología e innovación: Construyendo un futuro sustentable. Venezuela 2005-2030*. Caracas: MCT.
MED [Ministerio de Educación]. 2004. *La educación Bolivariana. Políticas, programas y acciones: 'Cumpliendo las metas del milenio'*. Caracas: MED.
MES [Ministerio de Educación Superior]. 2007. *Memoria y cuenta 2006*. Caracas: MES.
MF [Ministerio de Finanzas]. 2007. *Memoria y cuenta 2006*. Caracas: MF.
Mooney, Christopher P. 1986. Criteria for justice. *American Journal of Economics and Sociology* 45 (2): 223-33.
Muhr, Thomas. 2008. Nicaragua re-visited: from neo-liberal 'ungovernability' to the Bolivarian Alternative for the Peoples of Our America. *Globalisation, Societies and Education* 6 (2): 147-61.
Muhr, Thomas and Antoni Verger. 2008. Venezuela. In *The Developing World and State Education: Neoliberal Depredation and Egalitarian Alternatives*, ed. Dave Hill and Ellen Rosskam. New York: Routledge.
Muhr, Thomas and Antoni Verger. 2006. Venezuela: higher education for all. *Journal for Critical Education Policy Studies*, 4 (1), http://www.jceps.com/index.php?pageID=article&articleID=63.
O'Riordan, Timothy. 1993. The politics of sustainability. In *Sustainable Environmental Economics and Mangement*, ed. R. Kerry Turner, 37-69. London: Belhaven.
Pogge, Thomas. 2007. Why inequality matters. In *Global Inequality*, ed. David Held and Ayse Kaya. Cambridge: Polity.

RBV [República Bolivariana de Venezuela]. 2001. *Líneas generales del plan de desarrollo económico y social de la nación 2001-2007*. Caracas: RBV.
RBV. 2007. *Líneas Generales del Plan de Desarrollo Económico y Social de la Nación 2007-2013*. Caracas: RBV.
RBV. 2008a. *Aspectos sociales*.
Santos, Boaventura d.S. 2002. *Toward a new legal common sense*. London: Butterworths.
Schedler, George. 1978. Justice in Marx, Engels, and Lenin. *Studies in Soviet Thought* 18: 223-33.
Tabak, Mehmet. 2003. Marxian considerations on morality, justice, and rights. *Rethinking Marxism*, 15 (4): 523-40.
UBV. 2004. *Documento Rector*. Caracas: UBV.

---

1. See Muhr & Verger (2006; 2008) for analyses of education in neoliberal and revolutionary Venezuela; Muhr (2008) for Venezuela's counter-hegemonic globalization.
2. SISOV, at http://www.sisov.mpd.gob.ve/indicadores/GA0100800000000/ (accessed May 23, 2008).
3. Calculated from MES (2007, 10) and 'Min. Educación registra más de 13 milliones de personas en formación en el país', *ABN*, 16/05/2007, http://www.abn.info.ve/go_news5.php?articulo=92060&lee=6.
4. Education at a Glance, at http://go.worldbank.org/JVXVANWYY0 (accessed May 20, 2008).
5. *Bachiller* is a holder of the *bachillerato*, the Latin American/Spanish equivalent to A-Levels.
6. A second major institution in support of HEFA is *Misión Sucre*, which in 2007 offered 21 study programmes distinct to the local contextual characteristics and requirements. By 2006, 77% of the hitherto excluded 472.363 *bachilleres* of all ages, as nationally surveyed in 2003, exercised their right to HE in *Misión Sucre*, of which 57% were women (MES 2007, 116).

Navigating Art Education Across Three Domains: Cultural, Pedagogical And Political

Themina Kader
State University of New York at New Paltz, USA

Introduction

Coming from a multicultural background, and having been educated in predominantly Euro/Western systems and traditions, but schooled in and strengthened by my own cultural philosophies and aspirations, I have tried to navigate a tortuous trajectory in search of the elusive ideal in teaching teachers how to teach art to students of all ages.

My Kenyan teaching experience spanned a period of two decades in which art education morphed from a subject that was for the *talented* few to being a lifeline for students who advanced to making careers in art. Political exigencies in the early 1980s changed the Kenyan education system from being primarily British oriented to American structured and influenced. Art's position on the public schools' education ladder teetered and finally fell into seeming oblivion in public schools in the first three years of the new millennium. Supposedly, art did not meet set national expectations for development, economic or otherwise. Art education has taken me to various physical spaces and time in Kenya, Uganda, Europe, Asia, and the United States. Each of these countries and continents has had a significant impact on my thinking and how I view the teaching of art.

Over the years the tertiary education that I was fortunate to acquire has sharpened my sensibilities to issues of agency pertaining to and the rights and privileges of the marginalized populace of the non-Western art world, the anti-Islamic attitudes currently prevailing, and the biased and faulty information imparted in the name of multicultural art education in this country. These seemingly disparate experiences and situations coalesce for me to form a rich canvas of interconnectedness that under gird the local and the global of being an art educator.

It is said that teaching is a noble profession. After more than three decades what little nobility there was in teaching for me is replaced by serviceability. For services rendered, I receive a bi-monthly paycheck for which I must be thankful to my students for were it not for them I would not have a job. The professoriate, I think, bestows on its cadre a level of distinguishability that is both palpable and problematic. Among the great teachers of the world have been women and men who have, by all accounts, changed the lives of millions of people across many generations and cultures. Today, in the 21st century, the mere notion of making a change in a person's life by teaching, and art education at that, seems antiquated in the extreme and rather embarrassingly saccharine.

Social/Cultural

When I started teaching education was racially stratified in Kenya. As an Asian, an appellation given to all Indians from South-east Asia by the British in pre-independent Kenya, I taught Indian girls in a primary school. Public schools were segregated by gender then as they are today. We had an Indian woman as principal, but a male British inspector of schools who supervised you and pronounced your fitness to be promoted and tenured. The closer one was to the top position in an institutional hierarchy the whiter one was.

This narrative is viable only because my personal life is so inextricably entwined with my profession. I no longer teach in a primary or a high school. I am a college professor now. In order to fully appreciate this long journey, vis-à-vis art and art education, it is necessary for me to go back in time from Kenya's pre-independent and post-independent history, to 1994 when I came to the United States to go back to school.

Pedagogical/Experiential

Vast amount of literature exists on the subject of education in Kenya from its inception as a British Protectorate and 50 years prior to that when missionaries had already infiltrated Kenya. The primary purpose of missionaries and mission schools was to promote evangelism and schools were used to produce skilled labor for the settlers' farms and clerical staff for the colonial administration. Conversion to Christianity required unquestioned servility.

It is beyond the scope of this essay to delve more deeply into the complex relationship that was set in place by the imperial British government and missionaries vis-à-vis education that would be efficacious for Kenyans. Suffice it to say that in the years following the two World Wars several independent, church-controlled, and government schools were established in which, "the most intellectually able African could reach the very limits of their abilities" (Mutua, 1975, p. 60-61)

In the midst of this climactic situation, enter another dynamic, the Indians. The immigrant communities, who came to Kenya from India to build the railway linking the coast (Mombasa) to the interior (Kisumu) in 1891, unwittingly exacerbated an already inequitable situation (Brennan, 1999; Gupta, 1998). For more than 50 years public financing of education short changed African education, so that as early as the first decade of the 20th century the proportion of money spent on African education was less than that of the white race. Kenyans from the very onset recognized that education would liberate them from the yoke of colonialism, so they demanded an education that was similar to that given to the Europeans, Indians, and Arabs.

Art Education

The evolution of art education from craft to fine art did not materialize until well after mid-1960s in most public schools. Religious education was still the top priority for the missions and in secular education art education, as we know it today, was certainly not on the primary school curriculum. In secondary schools, although art fared a little better it was still on the lowest rung of the ladder to success and was sanitized of all traditional African beliefs and content. Historically, the 50s and the 60s could be considered as the heyday for art, art education, and artists with the greatest numbers of well educated, Kenyans artists among them, (Miller, 1975).

Facilities for the teaching of art in pre-independence Kenyan schools varied greatly. Church-controlled schools were better equipped in terms of qualified teachers, equipment, and materials. Government schools in urban centers (Nairobi, Mombasa, and Kisumu) had better facilities than rural areas. All art materials were imported from Britain and as such not within the means of most parents. The situation changed after Kenya became an independent republic in 1963.

Education in post-independence era was in a state of flux. The number of Kenyans who had acquired education in the West had increased and although the vestiges of a racially divided education had not been eradicated, increasingly Kenyans demanded an education that measured up to their expectations of what Kenya needed, an education that would take into account local conditions and local needs.

In 1963, when Kenya finally achieved independence, universal free primary education was still an unfulfilled dream. Schools that were exclusively for the European and Asian population were being integrated. Volumes have been written on how the government of Kenya has tackled this issue since 1965. What is relevant here is the impact the Certificate of Primary Education (C.P.E.) introduced into the Kenyan education system in 1965 and 1966 (King, 1975) as an entry-level examination to a secondary school, had on art education. Art was technically on the books along with Kiswahili, domestic science (home economics), practical agriculture, religious knowledge and handicrafts (art), but not taught at all in Grade Eight because it was one of the subjects not required in the examination and hence not taught. Teachers, under pressure to teach for tests, more often than not, used time allocated to teach art, for core subjects. A direct result of this was that at its most crucial stage art was sidestepped.

With the introduction of the American structured 8-4-4 system of education in January 1985, art as a subject on the curriculum underwent further changes. These changes reflected a greater contextual awareness. Students' artwork portrayed a personal experiential slant. Local, communal, and ethnic sensibilities came into play far more. It also created a situation that was far from being egalitarian or equal. While the school-going population had increased to a level that was, according to the many critics of this system, unsustainable and unproductive, there was a growing number of more "fortunate" young people who could afford to go into schools that were run by private funds, foreign embassies, churches, and communities. In these schools art is still taught according to the curriculum of the sponsoring country or affiliation.

While art was a teachable subject as an elective in secondary schools, but not examined in primary schools, it contributed greatly to the many doors that literally opened for those students who wanted to make careers in art. Sadly, in the waning decade of the 20th century, art's position on the public schools' education ladder teetered and finally fell into seeming oblivion in public schools in the first three years of the new millennium.

It is within the context of such a historical background that I started to pursue what I loved doing best, teaching art. But first I had to go to college, to the University of East Africa, Makerere in Kampala, Uganda, to learn to become an artist and an art teacher. Makerere was a wonderful experience. The students came from all across Africa south of the Sahara, Britain, and even the United States. The faculty was a mixed bag, but predictably, the Art School's top brass was a Scotsman from South Africa. The sculptor was a Ugandan and among the painters was a Shia Iranian who also taught Islamic art history, a Sunni Sudanese from Khartoum who inculcated in me a lasting love for printmaking, particularly intaglio.

At Makerere, I learned all about the elements and principles of art and design, became very conversant with the world of Euro/Western art. Much to its credit, the Art School invited visiting scholars, among them a West African art historian/sculptor, whose slide lectures revealed to me the esoteric world of classical African art. Makerere was the corner stone of what was to follow, a long stint teaching art in a high school in Kenya and onwards to the USA.

Thus, after five years of elementary and middle school teaching, and four years of college, I reentered the Kenyan education system, the first colored woman, to continue from where I had stopped, this time teaching high school art in an elite institution, established for the sons of British servicemen. I replaced a British male art teacher, and was recruited by a Kenyan principal. My first year at Lenana set the benchmark for a pattern of behaviors and attitudes I would encounter vis-à-vis my career. I had to prove myself every step of the way. That I had a degree in art from Makerere, at that time the best university in Africa, south of the Sahara (excluding apartheid South Africa), was not enough. As the only woman on the faculty I worked like the proverbial Trojan horse to achieve results which had to be and were better than those obtained by my predecessor.

Political/Religious

In 1994, I came to the United States as a returning non-traditional student. The dynamics of diversity, multiculturalism, and pluralism were very much at play but I was naïve enough to think that it would not affect me because its concomitant appendage, discrimination, had not started to gnaw at my confidence and spirits and its side effects were not discernible yet. I rejoiced in the knowledge that, having experienced nepotism teaching in Lenana School of the 1970s, I was now lucky to be a student free of all narrow-mindedness. Although being the only student of color in a vibrant but rural mostly white southern college would be unusual, being neophiliac by temperament, I thought my peers would welcome, physically and literally, a new face among them. Besides, as a graduate student, my worldview was far wider than the young twenty-something undergraduates. It was presumptuous of me, of course, to believe in that line of thinking and I was put in my place.

The university had a well-developed studio department. I was the only resident student in MA in Art Education. "What did I know about the fine arts?" was a refrain most art education students and educators, white or colored, have heard fairly frequently in this country. That was the problem. I was not an "artist." Never mind that I already had a first degree in the Fine Arts with a major in printmaking and painting. The virulence with which my work was discussed was so out of proportion to the criteria of the critiques in a printmaking course that I felt the need to explain my work. It was personal and experiential. As Dissananyake has said, "Losing appreciation of the richness of the experience only destroys one's credibility" (1995, p. 33).

My art was about the people of Kenya with whom I had worked and lived. Why did this happen? The problem with my work was that it was *different* and *unfamiliar*, so I became a threat to the male students' sense of superiority and privilege.

After completing the MA in Art Education in a southern university, I went east to a large research school for graduate studies in art education. Coming to the east coast, I was reassured, would be just fine, because the east was more diverse and liberal in outlook and more progressive. Heavy doses of art history courses in Christian religious art, neutralized by exposure to the glories of Islamic art, albeit in small measure, at Makerere had germinated in me a nascent desire to explore and examine more rigorously the correlation between two monotheistic religions and their artistic traditions. I envisioned its pedagogical implications and its value in terms of a more cogent understanding of the fundamental differences between secular and profane and sacred and religious art.

It was not to be. In no uncertain terms, a member of my doctoral committee alleged that I had gone to graduate school to proselytize and the proof of his allegation was couched in my research interest, a comparative study of Christian and Islamic religious art. Although September 11, 2001 hadn't come to pass yet, phobias associated with anything Muslim and how it would affect my professional life reared their vicious fangs as early as 1996. Being discriminated against became a daily reality. The raison d'être of being in a graduate school, to search for "truth," was just lip service for me. My peers, abetted by a couple of my instructors, silenced my voice by subtle bullying. I couldn't talk about who I am as a human being and how my culture intertwined with my religion has shaped my philosophy as an educator. As an international student I was always afraid that if I did not toe the line that I would be summarily discontinued from the program.

My teaching philosophy is rooted in multiculturalism and I recognize that in this country diversity has various names and takes various forms. In 2000 when I landed a tenure-track assistant professor's position in a mid-sized 4-year college in the mid-west, I thought that I was well prepared to start teaching in America. However, having been a minority always, I am very well attuned to receiving non-verbal cues about perceptions and adept at teaching under conditions that were designed for a mainstream society and over the years have become accustomed to making adjustments in my life to meet the "needs" of my students. Notwithstanding that my needs were never a part of this equation, as a new professor I immersed myself into fulfilling as many requirements of service, scholarship, and teaching as I could. But, my antennas were constantly being repositioned for better reception apropos art education in the college I was teaching. For these students the concept of diversity and multiculturalism extended to known differences among their own ilk; differences they could deal with. Since the college was so homogenous students in general rationalized their open hostility toward any kind of change, attitudinal or pedagogical, by believing that the status quo would always prevail and that students they would teach after graduating would be like them; that what they were taught in grade school was what they would continue to teach. This frame of mind was unsettling for me, because in Kenya most students I taught wanted to broaden their horizons and learning new things was exciting.

The new millennium and 9/11 changed forever the juxtaposition of American culture with the world, let alone Islam. I believe that as educators first and art educators specifically, it behooves us to inculcate in our students a generosity of heart that proffers not tolerance by sufferance but unconditional acceptance of different cultures based on the premise that there is no single "truth" and to enforce a "common denominator" to evaluate, discuss, and teach art is incompatible with the principles of multiculturalism (Dissanayake, 1995) There are many myths, misconceptions and misinformation attached to the concept of multicultural art education. And I admit to being hypersensitive about how non-Western cultures and their arts are represented in the curricula of schools in this country. On my visits to schools, I have observed that art lessons depicting diversity are very popular and art teachers are very enthusiastic about teaching such lessons. Most of these lessons are confined to a designated time of the year. For example, in February Black History Month alternatively called

African American History Month spawns an array of masks that bear very little if any resemblance to an authentic African mask.

October is Hispanic Heritage Month. *Cinquo de Mayo, Dios de los Muertos* (Day of the Dead) and *Piñata*, observed in May, November and December respectively, provides literally a rich smorgasbord of festivities from Mexico. To validate teaching such lessons a mention is made of what each of these occasions means to the Mexicans. Other seasonal festivals such as Halloween, Valentine's Day, Christmas, and various relatives' days are also on the menu of art activities. In predominantly Caucasian schools, by having laminated posters of, say, a collage or two by Romare Bearden, and Faith Ringgold's *Tar Beach*, invariably juxtaposed by the 14 ubiquitous posters of the elements and principles of design fulfill the national requirement for appreciation of human diversity and culture.

Making Egyptian mummies is an all-year round favorite so much so that it never occurs to teachers that death and mummification were rituals as sacrosanct as any funeral service in the Western world. Consider the following: *create their own mummy case using cut paper and a variety of materials and use symmetry in the creation of their mummy.* This procedure exemplifies the manner in which Egyptian mummification is taught in an art lesson.

The art of Islam is an uncharted territory in schools in America. Up until 9/11 Islam was hardly an issue of any kind. Muslim students went along with the mainstream. One exemplar of Islamic art that was much in vogue among art teachers for several years prior to 9/11 was M.C. Escher and "Islamic tile design," as if it were Escher's work that influenced and taught Muslim architects about tile design. Chronological accuracy was never questioned. After 9/11 and the run-up to the Iraq war demonizing anything Islamic was de rigueur and patriotic.

If religion is a divisive construct, then culture can sometimes circumvent these effects in unexpected ways. Here is an example. A tradition of body decoration, common in the Middle East, Pakistan, and India, has become very popular among some enterprising and enlightened teachers who have likened tattoos to henna painting and named it henna tattoos. The nomenclature is faulty because henna painting is not permanent so to call it "henna tattoo" does disservice to an equally rich and traditional practice of body decoration that has a long historical lineage in countries of the South-Pacific.

Thanks to Madonna and other icons of the silver screen, a plant *lawsonia inermis,* henna, has given the imprimatur for cross-cultural communication. So it has come to pass that I have had the pleasure and privilege to share my knowledge of henna painting with teachers and students alike. Henna Painting as a lesson is a non-threatening and user-friendly way of introducing a culture, Islam in this case. It brings together communities in the spirit of conviviality during festivals such as *Eid,* weddings, and birthdays and can be a "fun" activity as well.

Conclusion

I have a vision of what art education could be. For education to meet it societal, cultural, economical, spiritual, and moral imperatives, innovation and change, must of necessity be nurtured and maintained. Change, realistically, is never easy especially when political exigencies are at play, when it demands of us to make adjustments in our core beliefs. For the arts and art education, in particular, that is an ever-present dilemma. In a developing country like Kenya, traditional art was and contemporary art still is bio-behavioral in essence and very much a part of every day life. Sadly, art education in Kenyan public schools is considered an unaffordable luxury; in this country it is affordable only within the strictures of standards and statutes. In schools in the United States, a commonly held belief is that because art is about expressing oneself, students should be left free to do that. Art must entertain students and be fun. However these constructs, laudable as they are and have a place in children's artistic development, should not diminish art education's intrinsic values. As a universal visual language art has always been a chronicler and communicator of events. Its very universality can coalesce multifarious world-views in which no single Weltanschauung is better or worse, right or wrong, just different. In institutions of higher education, the philosophy of change, not just for change's sake, but how art educators are trained needs to become the modus operandi for the second decade of the 21st century.

References

Brennan, James.1999. South Asian nationalism in an East African Context: The case of Tanganyika 1914-1956. *Comparative studies of south Asia, Africa and the Middle East,* Vol XIX:2

Dissananye, Ellen. 1995. *What is art for?* ? University of Washington Press: Seattle, WA.

Gupta, Das. 1998. *South Asians in East Africa: Achievement and discrimination.* South Asia: journal of South Asian Studies

King, K. 1974. "Primary schools in Kenya: Some critical constraints on their effectiveness." In Court & Ghai (eds) *Education, society and development: New perspectives from Kenya.*Cambridge, MA: Cambridge University Press

Miller, Judith. Von D. 1975. *Art in East Africa: A contemporary guide to East African art.* Nairobi: Kenya: Africa Book Services.

Mutua, Rosalind.1975. *Development of education in Kenya 1846-1963.* East African Literature Bureau. Nairobi: Kenya.

Out and Abroad: GLBT Resources

Cory Young
Ithaca College, New York, USA

Introduction

Matthew Shepard, a self identified gay college student from Wyoming, was murdered senselessly in 1998 by Aaron McKinney and Russell Henderson, both of whom were filled with hatred for someone who was different. To bring their son's life to justice and honor his spirit, Shepard's mother and father began a crusade to continue the fight that Matthew started for social justice. They created the Matthew Shepard Foundation, which was devoted to "replacing hate with understanding, compassion, and acceptance," organized events on campuses across the U.S., and campaigned to persuade young students to vote on policies/programs to eliminate hate crimes (Arcadia University Bulletin, 2006, p.1). As one student recalled, Mrs. Shepard shared a story about how Matthew learned, "when he went to high school in Switzerland, that the world is made up of different cultures and individuals and that the diversity and richness of humanity made him optimistic and excited about life's potential" (Sideli, 2000, p. 2).

The ripple effect of this tragedy evoked intense reactions and responses and provided the catalyst in academe to reconsider past efforts and present labors to combat social injustices suffered by gay, lesbian, bisexual and transgendered students (Risner, 2005, p. 238). Activists and educators "seeking to understand intellectually the ways in which forms of inequality affect the constitution of diverse expressions of sexuality" reflectively and reflexively engaged in conversations about intersectionality of sexuality and social inequality "in order to influence positive forms of social change" in their classrooms (Shapiro & Purpel, 2005, p. ix). These individuals embodied acritical/queer pedagogy designed to expose and challenge dominant heteronormative ideologies and dismantle systems of oppression, discrimination and homophobia (Kumashiro, 2003; Makau, 1996; McNinch & Cronin, 2004; Risner, 2007; Shapiro & Purpel, 2005; Waldo, 1998).

The impact of Matthew Shepard's death is no doubt one of the most influential moments in academe, evident by the intellectual threads of conversation that emerged to combat social injustices in higher education. What was often overlooked in this tragedy however was his life as a student, and more specifically his experiences of being gay and studying/living abroad. Sexual cultures exist in every country and have different languages, politics, behaviors, ideologies, and so forth that may conflict with a student's home culture. Unfortunately, very few empirical studies exist that untangle the messy connection between sexuality, identity, citizenship, and education, thus, repeating the same pattern of structural violence that social justice educators and theorists strive to overturn. According to Dolby (2004), much research focuses on how sojourners learn language, their academic achievements, and personal growth, with limited understanding of students' struggle with their national and other identities. David Comp (2003), a researcher at the University of Chicago, compiled an annotated bibliography of articles on underrepresented populations that yielded the "need for more research specifically focusing on the experiences and outcomes of GLBT students studying abroad" (p. 1). To that end, this chapter will create a new thread of discussion to showcase study abroad programs that are socially just.

Theoretical Framework

The intersections between social justice, education, sexuality, and identity are traced in this section and form the basis for understanding the unique challenges that LGBT students face when studying abroad. Beginning with social justice, Bogotch (2000) drawing heavily from Dewey's (1904) individualistic perspective concluded that: social justice is processual, a means to an end; and meanings of social justice are fluid "based on the practical experiences of the participants" (p. 5). Thus, educational institutions should have more than one mission or goal, to "permit individuals to work individually as well as collectively towards different notions of social justice" (Bogotch, 2000, p. 9).

Connie North (2006) mapped different conceptual meanings of social justice and implications for educators (Fraser, 1997; Fraser & Honneth, 2003, O'Connor, 2001; Young, 1990). These theorists complicated the focus on unequal distribution of power and economic struggle, and shifted the ground to cultural groups struggling to be visible, to eradicate domination, and to be recognized (Fraser, 1997; cited in North). Such refocusing allows educators to recognize and challenge institutional structures and normative privileging of mainstream values that stigmatize and silence those who live in the margins.

Teunis and Herdt (2007), in Sexual Inequalities and Social Justice, emphasized the positionality of the researcher as well as the "cultural logic and cultural emotion created through sexual inequality . . . the cultural meaning systems and social practices of actors in sexual cultures and social formations . . . the real-world processes of inequality . . . that disrupt civic participation and thwart the full achievement of social and sexual citizenship" (p.2).

Others theorists investigated/interrogated social injustices from various standpoints including democracy in the global world (Enslin, 2006), an applied communication approach focusing on agency, empowerment and decision making (Frey, 1998; Makau, 1996), constituting self in spaces abroad (Ortiz, 2000; Razack, 2005), and higher education administration (Clark, Bouis, Subbaraman, & Balón, 2004; Perlis & Shapiro, 2001).

The second theoretical thread for this paper is the process by which a student develops his/her sexual identity while studying at a college or university. Evans and Herriott (2004) conducted an ethnographic study of campus climate for LGBT students, as a way of augmenting theories of identity development created by D'Augelli (1994) and Fassinger (1998), both of whom have been cited extensively in educational literature. D'Augelli argued that the development of an LGBT identity is a process, requiring an individual to move through six steps. Each step is influenced and informed by the person, the intimate relationships he/she has with others, and socio-cultural factors. Fassinger claimed LGBT people develop both an individual and group identity, and that these identities can manifest themselves at different times.

As Waldo (1998) and Dunlap (2002) observed many GLBT students explore their sense of self and come out in college and developmentally struggle with expressing their identity/ies as students and as sexual beings. This process does not take place in a vacuum and is further shaped by the institutional and local culture, both of which may or may not be accepting. Studying abroad can either increase the struggle or provide a moment in which the difficulties disappear, as explained in the next section.

Unique Challenges

"If there's anything that I learned this year, it was that I am me and I have to love myself for who I am. I can't depend on other people to help define me or tell me who I am . . . If I have learned one thing, it's that being me . . . whatever sex I choose to like that particular day is exactly who I will be." (Excerpted from Evans & Herriott, 2004, p. 323)

Colleges and universities in the United States that offer study abroad programs provide students with educational opportunities that "empower sojourners and promote their personal growth, including the acquisition of intercultural communication skills" (Frey, 1998, p. 159). Such programs can be organized around a specific topic, class, country, region, or time period (two week immersion, semester, academic year). Others are designed for challenging students' world views and broadening their horizons, literally and figuratively, thus helping individuals see things from different perspectives and become worldlier and well rounded.

An unintended assumption operating is a hierarchy of identity, in which an individual is first a student or member of the educational organization, then a citizen/representative of the US, and lastly, a person embodied with multiple intersecting social locations (sexual orientation, race, class, gender, etc). This hierarchy exists in a program's discourses/language, and in the priority given to specific topics during orientation like goals, finances, passports and visas and so on, evident on the Education Abroad website at Bowling Green State University:

> "Students who step outside their comfort zone to learn in cities and towns that are filled with unfamiliar peoples, traditions, and languages change in ways unknown to those who choose to stay behind. Those students who move forward build enormous self-confidence and gain the ability to see the complexity of how their own country fits into the world as a whole."

> "BGSU students will graduate to become the next generation of political leaders, educators, and scientists. In order for our nation to continue to thrive, our future leaders must know how to successfully participate in the globalized world of the present and of the future. The only way to gain this understanding is to communicate with people of other cultures, religions, beliefs and political perspectives, and experience life outside the borders of the United States."

> "Bowling Green State University recognizes the importance of globalized study and is committed to international education. By the year 2010, the University hopes 10 percent of its undergraduate students will study abroad. To encourage this, academic study abroad experiences bearing three or more credits will count as fulfilling the International Perspectives requirement for purposes of General Education (p.1)"

In this passage, students are treated as members of an aggregate, not as whole individuals with multiple social identities. This can create inevitable concern for GLBT students who, already silenced in other arenas, might at first glance not "see" themselves in this description.

A similar pattern can be seen in American University's Rome Enclave Student Guide Supplement. The table of contents contains twenty-two items such as program structure, housing, language, and social and cultural activities. GLBT issues are the second to the last to be discussed, in a total of two paragraphs:

> "Students will certainly find GLBT friendly places in Rome. Homosexuality is legal in Italy, but tolerance levels can be expected to vary. Italian legislation reflects a low level of concern with GLBT issues—not until 1999 was a bill proposed to include sexual orientation as a category in the anti-discrimination law. There is no legal acceptance of same-sex partnership, rights to succession in housing or social welfare."

> "GLBT students should carefully consider in what places and contexts openness about sexual orientation is safe. Helpful organizations include Arcigay & Arcilesbica Nazionale and Circolo Mario Mieli * as of April 2000 (emphasis added, p. 17)."

As students embark on the three phases of studying abroad—leaving home; making a home away from home; and going back home—gay, lesbian, bisexual, transgender students face dialectical tensions. In the first phase, traveling to another country can be either a liberating experience or a terrifying event, depending upon a number of variables: whether the student is out to him/her self and others, how *out* the person is, the level of acceptance in family/organizational/cultural environments, and/or legal constraints. Dunlap (2002) spoke to this, acknowledging that "studying in a place where no one knows you gives you a freedom of deciding if it is time to break from old expectations of family and friends. For some students, studying abroad can be a time to experiment with coming out" (p. 3). Leaving home creates a safe "third space," quoting Homi Bhabha (1994), in which an individual can express his/her sexuality in the absence of parental disapproval and conservative attitudes. Alternately, the same liberating experience can be a dangerous, legally punishable and constricting situation as definitions of sexuality, sexual identity, and relationships are fluid, culturally disparate, and less obvious in other contexts.

When making a home away from home, GLBT students face other difficulties related to host families, language, laws and legislation, and choices about health and safety, relationships (romantic or otherwise). As one student narrated, before embarking to Germany:

> "Contrary to many people, my discovery of being accepted to an Indiana University overseas program was not met with immediate joy, but with uncertainty and reservation. Here I had the opportunity to spend a year overseas studying in a German university in Hamburg . . . I tried to figure out why I wasn't jumping up and down screaming . . . See, the thing is I'm gay. Now, one may be wondering what that has to do with studying overseas for a year. There is no easy answer for that, but the quick answer is everything and nothing. Being gay did not affect my ability to speak German or my academic prowess, but it has quite a big effect on who I am. I knew that I would be going to live in a foreign country in a different culture, and that I would be spending quite a lot of intense time with about 20 other Americans, most of whom I did not know. How would my sexual orientation fit into all of that? I also knew that I would be leaving my sphere of family and friends who knew I was gay — my sphere of comfort. I know from just everyday living that coming out is a constant process, but this was like starting over almost from scratch." (Pitts, 2000)

"Recognizing the need to help LGBT students with these types of queries, the Center for Lesbian, Gay, Bisexual, Transgender Education and Outreach Services at Ithaca College (IC) in January 2006 published a pamphlet which included a section entitled "What I wish I knew then that I know now . . ." offering quotes from IC students who studied abroad:"For trans or genderqueer folks, consider ways to minimize the hassles when going through security checkpoints, what kinds of documents to keep with you in case you get stopped/harassed, etc."

"The language in my host country used a lot of gender-specific pronouns and endings on regular words and stuff, really different than the way we use language here. At first it freaked me out, not just because it was a lot to remember but because I am sometimes mistaken to be a different sex than I really am (both at home and abroad!). Then I noticed that my host family found a way to adapt — without even really talking about it directly, they kind of made up a new non-gendered "article word" that they used for me (instead of the traditional choice of the male or the female article words). At the time it just happened, but now I realize it was so cool!"

"Also, students should learn the laws specific to gay rights. Find out the proper and improper terminology for describing LGBT persons and relationships in the language. Is there a word that distinguishes a same-sex partner from a same-sex friend? What are the slang terms for LGBT persons? Are they appropriate to use? If so, when and with whom?"

Other students narrated stories around the same theme on the difficulty of understanding the cultural context for intimate behaviors like kissing and holding hands:

Mr. de Berry, the senior at San Francisco State . . . began dating a Spanish man. When they walked down the street, many people yelled 'Marcon!' (derogatory slang for gay man) at them. Once they sneaked a kiss in a park and were chased by two men who hurled threats at them (Rubin, 1997, p.2)

Joe Murnan, as part of a panel discussion at a conference in Philadelphia, revealed how the political and social culture of Korea, influenced his experiences of studying abroad as a gay male:

I first discussed the climate for GLBT students in Korea where I had lived and worked for 4 years. Before the Korean War, any mention of sex was taboo in Korean society. Public discourse on sexuality has really only started in the last ten to fifteen years, but there is still very little hard information about sexuality in Korea . . . Homosexuals have no established tradition of overtly discriminatory laws to struggle against. There are no sodomy laws proscribing oral or anal intercourse, largely because these acts have traditionally been considered utterly unmentionable in any public forum or documents. This may soon change. The number of homosexuals coming out of the closet is growing every day. Korea witnessed its first lesbian commitment ceremony on November 27, 1995 . . . I then went on to discuss GLBT issues for students from Moslem societies in the Arab World - Turkey, Iran, Pakistan and Afghanistan . . . In general, men are more intimate with each other than in the West. It is not uncommon to see male friends holding hands in public. It is also not uncommon to see men kiss each other on the cheeks during their greetings

. . . I also mentioned that punishment for same gender sexual encounters in these countries run the gamut of imprisonment not exceeding one year to public flogging and even death. In one country recently 9 young men were sentenced to up to 2,600 lashes and four to six years in prison for "deviant sexual behavior (Murnan, 2002).

The last phase of studying abroad occurs when the student re-enters his/her home country with established relationships intact despite the changes he/she has experienced. Reverse culture shock is disorienting to most students returning to their home country, but is compounded considerably for GLBT students. The Informal International Education Task Force on GLBT Concerns at the University of Minnesota published a document in 1993 for facilitators to help develop GBLT sensitive orientation materials. One of the areas addressed was Reentry that emphasized the need for students to be aware of the:

> "reentry adjustment and that this process may be intensified when a student has question his or her sexual identity . . . it is particularly important that they think about the ways they might have changed before they come home . . . One implication may be that family and friends may blame the study abroad experience for changes in the student, rather than acknowledging a lifelong identity." (p.3)

Ten years later, Dunlap (2002) reiterated this concern claiming, "Upon returning home these students may actually experience a painful re-closeting, returning to a life that they had all but left behind with limited or no support for the important growth they experienced overseas" (p. 3).

Socially Just Study Abroad Programs

So, you may be wondering, how does a study abroad program that is LGBT sensitive differ from a more conventional program? What makes these programs socially just? The answer lies in what Frey (1998, 1996) and Makau (1996) classify as an applied communication approach to social justice. According to Frey and his colleagues (1996) this approach is defined as "engagement with and advocacy for those in our society who are economically, socially, politically, and/or culturally under resourced" (p. 110). Central to engagement is to do research that privileges the agency of these under resourced individuals, and their democratic participation in decision making that helps to improve their lives.

How can these ideas be transferred or manifested from this context into study abroad programs? First, through reversing the identity hierarchy described in the beginning by privileging the GLBT part of a student's identity, and treating students not as an aggregate, but as individual with specific social locations; Second, by advocating and acknowledging the specific concerns faced by GLBT students; Third, by providing resources to assist them in making safe and healthier choices on their travels abroad.

Although several universities (Appendix A) address GLBT issues, the school that integrates all of the criteria above is Ithaca College. The pamphlet specifically created to address concerns of GBLT students is available at http://www.ithaca.edu/lgbt/assets/ studyabroad.pdf. The student's sexual identity is privileged first: "If you are a member of the LGBT community and you are interested in studying abroad, then you are taking the right step by reading this brochure" (2006, p.1).

Second, the Office of International Programs, and the Center for Lesbian, Gay, Bisexual, and Transgendered Education, Outreach and Services acknowledges the individual person and his/her own "set of circumstances in terms of their LGBT identity" that might emerge while studying abroad (p. 1).

Third, included in the brochure are a series of questions to be answered by students before making the decision to study abroad, in addition to helpful hints from previous students, and online resources. All are meant empower the individual to participate in the experience of studying abroad, and to make this experience safe and comfortable. To conclude this chapter, I would like to leave with a passionate plea by Dunlap (2002):

> "To understand how gay, lesbian, bisexual, and transgendered students' experiences abroad might be different is an important part of helping them. We can do this by informing ourselves about the process of identity development for GLBT students [and recognizing our biases] . . . We can take into account the country in question and the perceived climate for GLBT students . . . and realize that . . . students do not come to your office to give you an opportunity to work through your issues."

APPENDIX A
Other Schools and Organizations

Bowling Green State University, Brandeis University, Brown University, California State University at Chico, College of Saint Benedict and Saint Johns University, Colorado State University, Colorado University at Boulder, Indiana University, Michigan State University, North Dakota State University, Ohio State University, Penn State, San Francisco State University, Seattle University, Suffolk University, UMBC, an honors university in Maryland, University of Illinois, University of Massachusetts, Amherst, University of Minnesota, University of Nevada Las Vegas, University of Wisconsin, Madison.

National Organizations

Amnesty International: LGBT Network
IGLHRC—International Gay and Lesbian Human Rights Commission
ILGA—International Lesbian and Gay Association
ISA—International Studies Abroad.
NAFSA—Association of International Educators Rainbow Special Interest Group
National Consortium of Directors of LGBT Resources in Higher Education.

References

American University. *"AU Abroad Italy: Rome Enclave Student Guide Supplement."* http://auabroad.american.edu/enclave/index.cfm.

Arcadia University *"Vote—and Make a Statement, Says Judy Shepard."* University Bulletin, October 24, 2006. http://gargoyle.arcadia.edu/bulletin06fall/1024.htm.

Bhabha, Homi. K. *The Location of Culture*. London: Routledge, 1994.

Bogotch, Ira. E. *"Educational Leadership and Social Justice: Theory into Practice."* Paper presented at the annual meeting of the University Council for Education Administration. Albuquerque, NM, 2000. Retrieved from Educational Resources Information Clearinghouse (ERIC) database: No. ED 452 585.

Clark, Christine, Bouls, Gloria, J., Subbaraman, Sivagaml, and Balón, Daniello." Diversity Initiatives in Higher Education: Social Justice from Classroom toCommunity". *Multicultural Education* 12, no.2 (Winter 2004): 55-59.

Comp, D. "The Current State of Research on GLBT Students StudyingAbroad." *Lesbigay SIGnals* 9, no. 2 (Spring, 2003):1-2. http://www.indiana.edu/~overseas/lesbigay/vol9_2/92research.html.

D'Augelli, Anthony. R. "Identity Development and Sexual Orientation: Toward a Model of Lesbian, Gay, and Bisexual Identity Development," *Human Diversity: Perspectives on People in Context*, eds. Edison. J. Trickett, Roderick Watts, and Dina Birman (San Francisco: Jossey-Bass, 1994), 312-333.

Dolby, Nadine. "Encountering an American Self: Study Abroad and National Identity." *Comparative Education Review* 48, no. 2 (May 2004): 150-173.

Enslin, Penny. "Democracy, Social Justice, and Education: Feminist Strategies in a Globalizing World." *Educational Philosophy and Theory*, 38, no.1 (2006):57-67.

Evans, Nancy. J and Herriott, Todd. K. "Freshman Impressions: How Investigating the Campus Climate for LGBT Students Affected Four Freshman Students." *Journal of College Student Development* 45, no. 3 (2004, May/June): 316-332.

Fassinger, Ruth. E. Lesbian, Gay, and Bisexual Identity and Student Development Theory. In *Working With Lesbian, Gay, Bisexual, and Transgender College Students: A Handbook for Faculty and Administrators*, ed. Ronni. L. Sanlo (Westport, CT: Greenwood Press, 1998), 13-22

Fraser, Nancy. *Justice Interruptus: Critical Reflections on the "Postcolonial" Condition*. New York: Routledge, 1997.

Fraser, Nancy and Honneth, Axel. *Redistribution or Recognition? A Political-Philosophical Exchange*, trans. J. Golb, J. Ingram, and C. Wilke. (New York: Verso, 2003).

Frey, Lawrence. R. "Communication and Social Justice Research: Truth, Justice, and the Applied Communication Way." *Journal of Applied Communication* Research (May 1998): 155-164.

Frey, L. R., Pearce, W. Barnett., Pollock, Mark. A., Artz, Lee, and Murphy, Bren. A. O. "Looking For Justice in All the Wrong Places: On a Communication Approach to Social Justice." *Communication Studies*, 47 (Spring/Summer 1996): 110-127.

Kumashiro, Kevin. K. "Queer Ideals in Education". Co-published simultaneously in Journal of Homosexuality, 4 no. 2/3/4: 365-367; and in *Queer Theory and Communication: From Disciplining Queers to Queering the Discipline*, eds. Gus. A. Yep, Karen. E. Lovaas, John. P. Elias (New York: Haworth Press: 365 367.

Makau, Josina M. "*Notes on Communication Education and Social Justice.*"Communication Studies, 47 (Spring/Summer 1996): 135-141.

Martino, Wayne. "Book Review: I Could Not Speak My Heart: Education and Social Justice For Gay And Lesbian Youth." *Canadian Journal of Education* 28, no. 3 (2005): 549- 554.

Murnan, John. *LGBT Issues in Many Cultures.* http://www.indiana.edu/~overseas/lesbigay

North, Connie E. 2006. "More Than Words? Delving Into the Substantive Meaning(s) of "Social Justice" In Education." *Review of Educational Research* 76, no. 4 (Winter): 507-535.

O'Connor, Alice. 2001. *Poverty, Knowledge: Social Science, Social Policy, and the Poor in Twentieth Century U.S. History*. Princeton, NJ: Princeton University Press.

Ortiz, Anna M. "Expressing Cultural Identity in the Learning Community: Opportunities and Challenges." *New Directions for Teaching and Learning* 82 (Summer,2000):67-79.

Perlis, Susan M. and Shapiro, Joan P. 2001. "Understanding Interconnections Between Cultural Differences: A Social Justice Imperative For Educational Administrators."Paper presented at the UCEA Conference in Cincinnati, Ohio. November 2,. Retrieved from Educational Resources Information Clearinghouse (ERIC) database: No. ED 467730.

Pitts, Matt. Study Abroad Student Perspective. http://www.indiana.edu/~overseas/lesbigay

Pratt, Mary. L. *Imperial Eyes: Travel Writing and Transculturation*. New York: Routledge, 1992.

Razack, Narda. ""Bodies On The Move": Spatialized Locations, Identities, and Nationality in International Work," *Social Justice* 32 no. 4 (2005): 87-104.

Risner, Doug. "What Matthew Shepard Would Tell Us: Gay and Lesbian Issues iEducation," in Critical Social Issues in American Education: Democracy and Meaning in a Globalizing World, 3rd ed. Volume in the *Sociocultural, Political,and Historical Studies in Education Series*, eds. H. Svi Shapiro

and David E. Purpel (Mahwah, NJ: Lawrence Erlbaum Associates, 2005), 237-251.
Rubin, Amy M. Some Study Abroad Programs Start to Consider Needs of Gay Students. *Chronicle of Higher Education* 44, no. 10 (October 31, 1997): A53- 55. Retrieved March 3, 2007 from LexisNexis database.
Shapiro, H. Svi and Purpel, David. E., eds. Critical Social Issues in American Education: Democracy and Meaning in a Globalizing World. 3rd ed. Mahwah, NJ: Lawrence Erlbaum Associates, 2005. Volume in the *Sociocultural, Political, and Historical Studies in Education Series.*
Sideli, Kathleen. *The Legacy of Matthew Sheppard.* http://www.indiana.edu/~overseas/lesbigay
Teunis, Niels and Herdt, Gilbert, eds. *Sexual Inequalities and Social Justice.* Berkeley, CA: University of California Press, 2007.
Waldo, Craig R. "Out on campus: Sexual orientation and academic climate in a university context." *American Journal of Community Psychology* 26, no. 5(1998): 745-774.
Young, Iris. M. *Justice and the politics of difference.* Princeton, NJ: Princeton University Press, 1990.

Teacher Training and Social Justice

Drama and Social Equity in Teacher Education Programs In Palestine

Hala Al-Yamani
Bethlehem University, Palestine

Introduction

Education is a major influence in the process of change, development and renewal. It can be liberating, fostering new perspectives, attitudes, thoughts, feelings and bodies of knowledge that can enhance lives of human beings and create social justice, or it could play the opposite role, creating social injustice. The broader societal patterns of injustice are often reflected in the educational system: unequal power relation concerning race, religion, gender, disabilities, and age manifest themselves in schools as elsewhere.

This is very obvious in Palestine. Palestinian society is still patriarchal and hierarchical. In a traditional society such as Palestine, education and knowledge, as the most important tool for bringing about changes in values and attitudes, is not effective, among the upcoming younger generations, because it is rooted in traditional thinking.

In schools, teachers work to provide and check knowledge that students must memorize. The underlying assumption of these teachers is that school is a place solely to provide learners with knowledge that is absorbed uncritically. This approach views learning as memorization of information rather than the ability to discover, master, and use knowledge to make meaning of and improve quality of life.

Kumashiro (2004) has explained that sometimes school becomes the agent for spreading various forms of oppression particularly when it includes only certain materials organized into certain disciplines, prepares teachers using certain methods, and treats students in certain ways. This reflects the need to develop new educational methods that present students with new values and attitudes towards themselves as individuals as well as towards others. It reflects the need for education to become more liberal and humanistic in dealing with both teacher and learner. Teachers must be highly qualified and trained in ways which can make a real difference to their students in the classroom. A teacher of true humanity can make the educational process interesting, challenging, and innovative and can, I contend, be the agent of change in society and work on achieving social equity.

In my view, drama as a subject instead of process in teacher education programs constitutes an important tool to develop all these areas and bring change into the classroom and in the long term, in society. What is drama and how can drama achieve social equity? Before answering these questions it is important to discuss the training of teachers and social equity.

Training Teachers And Social Equity

Most researchers on social equity emphasize three issues. These include:
Cultural Knowledge
Teachers should have knowledge of the social and cultural contexts that shape education as well as knowledge of the role of culture in mediating learning (Smith 2004). In order to work effectively with diverse populations, teacher-training programs must provide opportunities for the trainees to study and research topics related to racial discrimination, religious intolerance, gender equity, economic bias, and other forms of oppression. This prepares them to deal openly with their students as unique individuals.

Reflection and Critical Thinking Skills
It is important to stimulate thoughts and beliefs of future teachers and to push them to think fully of issues related to their lives and to the life of other people. Teacher training professionals must provide them with opportunities to ask "how did things come to be the way they are and for what reasons?" (Owens 2007). Learning is dealing with personal knowledge and life matters by focusing fully on them and trying to reach other related aspects of it. Developing critical skills can provide answers to questions of oppression and how teachers and education are supporting oppression or working against it.

Self Identity
Self-inquiry is a critical component of future teachers' education since it works on discovering their social identities, which leads to an understanding of themselves (Solomon 2005). Teachers need to be challenged in order to question their own beliefs, values, biases and prejudices so as to achieve self-conscious awareness (Vincent 2003). Spaces need to be created in which teachers can interrogate and reflect upon their own attitudes and prejudices, as a step towards helping others initiate change and development of a fairer and more equitable society. Drama provides this space. Drama as an art form and a teaching meth-

odology can embody these concepts and help the trainees to understand who they are and what they value in teaching.

What is Drama?

Drama is not a newly discovered activity in education and historically it has taken two main forms:
- as an integrative method in the teaching of different subjects
- as a subject in its own right, where the emphasis is on acquiring the skills of drama as a medium of expression.

In this essay I deal with drama as the first form. In its integrative form, drama is based on the premise that everyone can act, and can learn from his or her experience of the activity. In the capacity to act 'as if', the person is in a different situation or he or she is playing another character; both states presuppose the use of imagination. In the imaginative process the person in the role of the other is still employing his own thoughts, feelings, attitudes, movements and gestures (Wollheim 1973). The participants are part of the experience, experiencing themselves in a different world and showing a kind of inner life. Through this process people express deep feelings and come face to face with themselves in the dramatic process by comparing the 'self' with the 'other'. They enter into the social, cultural and political fabric and they try to follow its warp and weft to understand what it is and how it came to be.

It is a process where the person is engaged in 'practice living' as Way (1967) described it. In practice living through various dramatic activities individuals transcend time, place, and the people who are related to that time and place; they might even go beyond the self as in playing roles different from those played in ordinary daily life.

I decided therefore, to begin with a pilot project to follow the development of pre-service teachers in the Early Childhood Programs and to study the possibilities of using drama as a teaching method.

Methodology of the Research

In this project I worked with 15 students in their first and second years of college. I developed three courses, *Drama for Teachers of Young Children, Introduction to Early Childhood Education* and *Palestinian Family*.

I developed various drama activities, which focused on the content of the courses. Drama activities were related to play and warming up activities, imagination, concentration, tableaux, mime, planned and unplanned improvisation and role-play. I focused my research on studying drama as an educational experience with those students, and whether it helps them in developing themselves. How and in which areas does it affect them? In conducting this research, I wished to study all students who registered to take Drama for Teachers of Young Children course and who took the other two courses.

The type of questions I asked and the issues that I wanted to understand could only be achieved by using qualitative research methods. The process of understanding and giving a meaning to what was going on in these sessions, which was part of my experience as a researcher, is called an 'interpretative approach'.

I used the following tools in collecting the data:

- Observations by two assistants who joined all sessions and generated documented data of the student's interaction and reaction.

- Interviews: three different interviews conducted by assistants who used open-ended questions focused on students' description of their experience with drama.

- Students' Journal: participants wrote their own reflections on the individual sessions for the three courses.

- My Journal: Ongoing classroom observations and research reflections were recorded through daily writings in my Journal.

Drama And Social Equity

In general the common elements between the different sources of the data provided two main points:

1. It revealed the nature of the challenges faced by students with drama as a learning medium especially in the early period of the courses. These challenges reflected the particular qualities of the culture, such as low self-confidence, lack of communication skills and limited social skills. Many of the students felt "silly and funny" when they acted or participated in specific activities. They struggled initially with the drama activities in relation to their culture, which had conditioned them firmly to control their actions both toward themselves and toward others. This was expressed strongly by one of the students who reflected the views of others:

> "Drama included new and very different ideas, which were taboo in society and conflicted with my own ideas that I had learned from society. I felt it was wrong, as mature women, to do some aspects of the drama work. It was so difficult for me to imitate children and animals. I am an adult and I should act in a mature and responsible way." (Third Interview, KAOT, 2004)

2. The open interaction as a whole person was a big challenge for most of the students. I discovered lack of self-confidence and the difficulty in moving and acting freely by most of the students. This is what I wrote in my Journal.

> "When I saw the level of participation in the different activities especially those based on using and moving the body, I was astonished. Some of them were simply unable to do some of the movements.... I had thought that these were basic skills which would present no problem, however, very few of the students were able to accomplish this, or enjoy the activity. This was totally unexpected.

These students are young- 19-20 years- yet they behaved like middle-aged people." (2004)

I realised how inadequate the traditional system of education was in developing personal aspects of the students and the lack of dealing with them as a whole unit. Second, it showed good evidence of the effect of drama as a medium that would enable students to interact on an intrapersonal and interpersonal levels. It helped them develop professional skills related to their role as future teachers. Drama helped students develop as teachers by increasing their self-awareness, by encouraging critical thinking and by inculcating new attitudes and behaviours. I will enumerate on each of these below.

Self-Awareness

Experiences in drama can facilitate a great deal of personal and psychological liberation and understanding of self. It can play an effective role in shaping personal identity (Young 2000). Drama as a medium helped students to discover themselves as people. The various activities stimulated them to discover, think about and understand themselves:

> "I recognised things that I had never noticed about myself and that I only discovered through taking part in these activities. Sometimes I ask myself: am I really like this?" (Journal, MITO, 2004)

Drama provides opportunities for trying out all sorts of ideas, dreams, hopes and fears and all sorts of conflicts, without feeling fearful or threatened since, in the drama experiences, people generally inhabits a fiction.

> "I discovered a great deal about myself. There were many things I already knew but I had never tried to find out why they were there or to find out more. For example, why I felt hesitant in discussions with other people. Is it to do with self-confidence or what? I wanted to develop this in order to become an independent and responsible person who would be a good future mother and teacher. Drama helped me to know many things related to my childhood. How was it? How had people treated me?" (Third Interview, SAQI, 2004)

Drama activities provided students with an opportunity to think deeply about themselves, and to develop themselves. One student wrote:

> "I discovered myself as well as different characteristics that I developed. For example, I discovered that I am careless and I do not pay attention to other people when they do things. I have no skills of observation and concentration. I am not bold, but drama helped me to be developed and to take action in developing myself." (Journal, GHAS, 2004)

They could recognize their value as humans with special gifts and talents. This was very clear in their description of drama experience, one student said:

"...before drama I was like a very valuable treasure, but covered with dust so nobody could see the signs of its beauty and value. Drama has swept the dust away and revealed the beauty of this treasure." (Second Interview, KAOT, 2004)

It helped them to think of themselves as teachers and reflect on the role of the teacher. They asked questions of themselves related to this and sometimes they answered these questions revealing that they expected the sort of interaction they were experiencing in drama to be mirrored in their interaction with pupils based on what they discovered within themselves. One student wrote:

"How will I deal with children who are imaginative while I have limited imagination? In addition, I cannot express my thought well as my thinking is not flexible. This will affect the children's belief in me as their teacher. How would I work on developing their imagination while I cannot do it or express it? Therefore, in future I will be a directive teacher who does not accept new ideas." (Journal, DIJA, 2004)

This reflects the strong impact of drama on the students, its positive effect and how it touched them as people and as future teachers. Drama as an experience might provide an opportunity for the person to start taking action in 'reorganising self' as Wright (2000) described it. He believed that learning contained in drama has two interrelated aspects: first, embodied experience, and second, reflective explanation of experience, which includes communication. Through reflective consciousness, abstract thought, and considerations about language use, a person builds a system of self-organisation.

Deep and Critical Thinking

The various tools reflected some development in the critical faculties of the students. They began to discuss matters related to their society, school, and family. They thought about the context of the dramatic experience. Their awareness moved further to recognition of their culture and society, which together restrain the individual from developing and feeling free.

"In our customs and traditions we lose the freedom of self-expression and the right to have an opinion. Otherwise we might become either an idiot or a rude person. Our society does not care about children nor recognise the importance of childhood. The most important thing is preparing her/him for future. They give great care to some aspects, but not to the child as a whole person." (Journal, SAQI, 2004)

They discussed matters related to the position of the child in society and criticized the values and the way boys and girls are treated differently. They discussed it and became much more aware of it from their position as adults and of the child as a developing entity. They became much aware of the actions of the teachers towards children in schools, a student said:

"... teachers treat children as objects, rather than human beings. They do not recognize the nature of children and they deal with them harshly." (Second Interview, SUSA, 2004)

This develops originality and deeply held personal aspirations that are important for full development. In the process of drama, participants start looking for reasons and results in actions and interactions of the self and the other. Carasso (1996) calls such an investigation a *dialogue*, and Heathcote (1984), refers to it as *negotiation*. It starts with an internal dialogue and progresses to external dialogue when the person deals with others.

New Attitudes and Feelings

Students discussed their emotional development since in drama, they were assuming different roles under different circumstances. They talked about dealing with other people with sensitivity and respect. Drama experiences helped them to understand the world of the child and how she/he is learns and adapts to her/his environment. They wrote about how they understood children's needs and how to act towards them in ways that would satisfy their needs:

"Now I understand some actions of children, which I did not understand before... Through my personal experience I understood reasons that make the child feel embarrassed in front of his peers, especially when he is finding it difficult to do things, which other children are doing easily. Now I could understand some feelings of the child that are important for me as a teacher." (Journal, MAHA,2004)

Being involved in the drama helped those students understand the child as a learner as well as a human being. It succeeded in changing students' attitudes of the child as a learner, as well as towards themselves as teachers. One student wrote:

"These experiences made me respect children regardless of who they are which was something new for me. I respected their needs. In the past I used to prefer good pupils either in their study or behaviour and I ignored quiet children. I looked at children from only one perspective but now I believe that they all have their own abilities and I should respect it. I could not see that before." (AMSH, Journal,2004)

In drama "the other" becomes a mirror that reflects "the person" and the person is able to see the self and to enter the world of the other. In this process a person gets a good opportunity for setting ideas by using narration related to the life of other people or to their life to try and experience what it means to be human in many different situations.

"I have learned how to deal with others. I have learned how to act with them in sensitive way, avoiding causing harm to any of them. I became able to understand the emotions and feelings of others by looking at their faces and dealing with them accordingly." (Journal, KAOT, 2004)

Putting themselves in the position of others made them more "sensitive", and able to understand the lives of others and therefore brought them closer to others and to children

> "I listened to every student and her story. In this activity I felt that I could live any situation and be affected by it, if it was sad then I felt sad and if it was happy then I felt so happy... I could empathise now with other people, not just my people as Palestinians, but also with others.... I could put myself in their shoes and feel their feelings and recognise their thoughts."(Journal, INSU, 2004)

Drama helped them distinguish feelings and interactions of others through their own experiences. In this way drama could be very helpful to future teachers to provide a good and supportive educational environment where students are comfortable and able to learn actively what they are studying. It developed those basic concepts for teachers to be able to play an effective role in schools and to create a stimulating environment and positive, human relationships with their students

Conclusion

To make a significant difference on a broad scale in Palestine, individual efforts must be joined by collective and institutional changes. At all three levels, teacher education programs have a critical role to play in creating social justice and equity in schools. They can do so by offering in-service and future teachers courses and other educational experiences that focus on questions of equity and diversity and that challenge stereotypes about various people. What they learn in their teacher education programs can have an enormous impact on the attitudes and practices that teachers bring with them to the schools where they work

Teacher programs should prepare humane teachers who are able to deal with and understand all people regardless of their backgrounds. Teachers who are fully aware of their role as change agents and who are active in creating just educational environment, participate in creating a just and better society. The promise of social justice and equal educational opportunity for all is still a deceptive dream in our world. It will be closer to becoming a reality by using proper educational directions and methods that integrate art as a way to develop a whole creative, critical, and sensitive human being.

References

Barrow, R. 1988. "Some observations on the concept of imagination," In *Imagination and Education* eds., Egan Kieran & Nadaner, Dan, Milton Keynes, Open University.

Carasso, Jean-Gabriel. 1996. "Identity and dialogue", In *Drama, Culture and Empowerment* (ed.), John, O'Toole & Kate, Donelan. Brisbane: IDEA Publications.

Gordon, Edmund W. 1999. *Education and Justice: a View from the Back of the Bus*, New York: Columbia University, Teachers College Press.

Heathcote, Dorothy, O'Neill, Cecily and Johnson, Liz. 1984., *Collected Writings on Education and Drama*, London: Hutchinson Education.

Holzer, Madelaine, 2005. "Many layered multiple perspective: aesthetic education in teaching for freedom, democracy, and social justice", In *Teacher Education for Democracy and Social Justice* (ed.), Nicholas M ,Michelli, & Francis L Keiser, New York: Routledge, Taylor &Francis Group.

Kumashiro, Kevin, 2004. *Against Common Sense: Teaching and Learning Toward Social Justice*, New York and London: Routledge Falmer.

Keiser, David L. 2005. "Learners are widgets: teacher education for social justice during transformational times", In *Teacher Education for Democracy and Social Justice* (ed.), Nicholas M ,Michelli, & Francis L Keiser. New York: Routledge, Taylor &Francis Group.

Libman, Karen. 1996. "Right from the Start: an initial drama session for preservice teachers", In *Drama Matters*, 1:1, 13-34.

Michelli, Nicholas M. & Keiser, Francis L. 2005. *Teacher Education for Democracy and Social Justice* (ed.), New York: Routledge, Taylor & Francis Group.

Owens, Allan , *Informing Pedagogy*, Chester University, United kingdom, 2007, unpublished article.

Smith, Marilyn C. 2004, *Walking the Road: Race, Diversity and Social Justice in Teacher Education*, New York: Teachers College Press.

Solomon, R. 2005. "The discourse of denial: how white teacher candidates construct race, racism and 'white privilege". *Race Ethnicity and Education*, 8:3.

Vincent, Carol. 2003. *Social Justice, Education and Identity*, London: Routledge Falmer.

Way, Brian, 1967. *Development Through Drama*, England: Longman.

Wollheim, Richard, 1973. *On Art and Mind* (Essays and Lectures, London: Allen Lane.

Wright, David, 2000. "Drama education: a 'self-organizing system' in pursuit of learning", *Research in Drama Education*, 5:1, 58-85.

Yamani, Hala, 2004. *The role of drama in initial teacher education: a study of drama's use in early childhood teacher education programs at Bethlehem University, Palestine*, a dissertation submitted to Exeter University in Partial fulfillment of requirements for the degree of Doctor of Philosophy.

Young, David L., 2000. "Reality drama: the drama classroom as a place for disclosure", *NADIE Journal*. 24:1, 75-94.

Measuring The Extent To Which Teachers Interpret Their Role In Educational Terms

Nwachukwu Prince Ololube
University of Port Harcourt, Nigeria
&
Daniel Elemchukwu Egbezor
University of Port Harcourt, Nigeria

Introduction

The world needs more and better teachers because of advances in global development. Teacher quality is an issue in most countries because many teachers are untrained or under-qualified (UNESCO, 2001). The effectiveness of any educational system depends upon the degree of expertise of the teachers. How successful teachers will be depends largely on how well they are prepared for their roles within the system. Teachers provide instruction as well as evaluate the educational progress of their students.

For example teachers teaching, assessing, and evaluating the progress made by students with special needs create a great challenge within an educational system. Students' progress is the result of instructional strategies employed in the classroom. Teachers must know how to evaluate the progress made by outstanding children as well as those who are not coping in meeting the set standards. Thus, teachers need to have specialized training and knowledge in both instructional competence and evaluation methodology within their professional background to be able to cope with the day-to-day details of pedagogical encounters with students. Competencies do not just refer to tasks; they must be associated with the characteristics and backgrounds of the person involved in them. The notion of competence goes beyond skills to include attitudes and stamina needed to carry action (even) through difficult circumstances (Husu, 2006).

Teachers' Role

Teachers' work with students who are actively planning and managing their futures; ideally, preparing students for a range of career pathways and helping them develop skills, habits, and attitudes they will retain over a lifetime of learning. The role of teachers has changed and continues to change from being instructor to becoming constructor, facilitator, coach, and creator of learning environments (UNESCO, 2002). Teachers play a vital and an increasingly more challenging role in the education of children. Teachers are successful in meeting these complex expectations because are aware of the appropriate teacher roles in different situations and have the personality skills that allow them to adapt to changing situations in a classroom (Campbell et al., 2004).

However, teachers' choices and actions of what they should do when there are so many competing circumstances and possibilities depend on a set of core ideas and roles such as developing and adopting routines and short cuts, internalizing classroom decision-making, and reducing the range of possible ways of thinking to manageable proportions (Eraut 1994, p. 70). On some occasions teachers request that their students be seen by psychologists in order to establish or negotiate a particular problem that is not the purview of the professional skills of teachers. Such teachers see themselves as making a crucial contribution to the identification of students' special needs (Armstrong, 1995).

Professional knowledge is regarded as a necessary component of a competent teacher's action (Husu, 2003). Pedagogical content knowledge refers to the knowledge and understandings, skills and dispositions, attitudes and beliefs that teachers consciously seek to improve their teaching competencies. It includes but is not limited to knowledge of and about particular subjects, pedagogical knowledge and skills, knowledge about children and learning, information about the social and political role of education, skill in organizing and managing classrooms, attitudes toward diverse learners and the dispositions of those learners to ask particular kinds of questions, (Shulman, 1986, 1987).

Clark (1986) attempt to understand teachers' knowledge traced the past development of teacher knowledge research and found three interconnected and partly overlapping phases in its development: 1. The teacher as a decision-maker—a teacher's task is to diagnose needs and learning problems of students and prescribe effective and appropriate instructional treatments for them. 2. The teacher as a sense-maker—decision-making was seen as one among several activities teachers perform. 3. The teacher as a constructivist—a teacher continually builds and elaborates his/her personal hypothesis of teaching and education.

Social and Classroom Interaction

Social and classroom interaction between teachers and students benefit students' learning process because it creates an environment for students to learn not in isolation but in a way that makes independent learning easier. Students follow instructions to complete a particular task. Vygotsky (1978) believed that social interaction is very important to the students' upbringing. Thus, effective interaction helps with the learning process because it adds additional framework and ideas to students' studies. According to Freiberg and Freebody (1995) teachers interacting with students not only meant encouragement and help to them, but also reminded them that they were not alone in their struggle to learn.

Teachers of tomorrow need a new approach to their job and a new vision of what it means to teach and learn. The challenge of introducing teachers at all levels and in all sectors to the necessary skills is immense, particularly at a time when technology applications continue to develop almost as fast as they can be taught (Jenkins, 1999). The effective use of varied instructional materials and constantly looking out for children with personal problems cannot be separated from attitudes and approaches to teaching and learning. Thus the role of teachers becomes one of initiating comparatively open approaches that seek to inspire, support, and smooth the progress of quality learning. Recent research (Campbell, *et al.* 2004; Ololube, 2005b) on teaching and learning appears to give particular emphasis to a deep knowledge of the subject to be taught and an understanding of and ability to use a range of pedagogical approaches. Teachers are also expected to have knowledge of the social development of children and of management function (Hämäläinen & Jokela, 1993). Teachers' role on the issue of quality in school is very vital and as such, teachers are regarded as prime movers in the improvement of that quality. That is why researchers persistently call for professional development of teachers, to reduce areas of waste and provide an effective means of improving quality in secondary schools (Ololube, 2005b).

Motivating Students

Motivating strategies arise because of specific beliefs and perceptions of the characteristics of individual students. To address students' emotional and motivational needs (Ololube, 2005a,) is to affirm that motivating them is an essential component of teaching and a critical issue in their educational development. Hardre and Reeve (2003) and Austin Dwyer and Freebody (2003) identified three important elements in students' motivation to learn
- the learning environment
- classroom instruction
- interpersonal interaction.

Some motivational elements at all these levels are generally within the teacher's control, and all of them can positively or negatively influence students' academic aspirations.

Students often fail to reach their full potential due to low motivation from teachers (Ololube, 2005a). Institutional and cultural factors (Niederhauser 1997, 98) related to a country's education system, and the structures of power are important examples of motivation or lack thereof, and high student achievement. Cheng (1994, pp. 221-239) defined power base as the use of reward power, coercive power, position power, and personal or professional power in the classroom to ensure students' compliance. Researchers especially in Africa and Asia see power as a valuable tool for effective teaching and high student academic achievement (Cheng, Cheung & Tam, 2002, pp. 138-155). However, to motivate unmotivated students, teachers should recognize that even when students use self-defeating strategies such as withholding effort, cheating, procrastination, their goal is actually to protect their sense of self-worth (Lumsden, 1994; Raffini, 1993).

Teachers' Motivation and Job Satisfaction

Motivation is the degree of readiness of an organization to pursue some designated goal and implies the determination of the nature and locus of the forces inducing the degree of readiness (Lewis, Goodman & Fandt 1995; Golembiewski, 1973, p. 597). Motivation has to do with the forces that maintain and alter the direction, quality and intensity of behavior. The liveliness of an organization, whether public or private, comes from the motivation of its employees, albeit their abilities play a crucial role in determining their work performance. Employee motivation is the complex of forces, drives, needs, tension states, or other mechanisms that start and maintain voluntary activity directed towards the achievement of personal goals (Hoy and Miskel, 1987, p. 176; Kelly, 1974, p. 279). From the above definitions some issues are brought to mind that deal with what starts and energizes human behavior and how those forces are directed and sustained as well as the outcomes they bring about.

Teachers' motivation and job satisfaction can be studied through several broad approaches *vis-à-vis* content or need based theories, process theories, and reinforcement theories. However, "employee motivation" is a complex and difficult term to define and its concept somewhat elusive, as the notion comprises the characteristics of the individual and situation as well as the individual's perception of that situation (Ifinedo, 2004; Rosenfield & Wilson, 1999).

Cushman's (1998) study on teachers' motivations and satisfactions found that often teachers speak of emerging from the isolation of their classrooms into partnerships, teams, and networks marked by collaboration among peers. Such initiatives have their tensions and costs, and at every stage of their careers teachers require explicit supports to carry them out, but they also yield intellectual and personal rewards that often renew their energy and commitment to continuing in a profession under siege.

Research Objectives

This chapter records the findings of a research study that reviewed and codified what had been already learned regarding teachers' attitudes and behaviors as they reflect students' academic achievement (SAA) which is the focal point for school effectiveness and quality improvement (Creemers, 1994). The study examined the role of both teachers and students within a school setting and how teachers used their knowledge of supposed roles to gain control and create meaning in their professional setting.

Method

The Instrument

The instrument used to collect data for this study was adapted from Cohen and Manion (1994) as constructed by David Marsland. The scale measures the extent to which teachers interpret their role in 'educational terms' or 'academic terms' in using different 'locational markers;' it gives a more representative picture of the respondent's orientation to his or her role and in so doing illustrates the principle of triangulation in a simple form. The advantages of this scale include its inexpensiveness, ease of use, and its encouragement of reflective enhancement of consensus. For example, one item or 'locational marker' by itself will tell us very little about a teacher's attitude but ten such related items or 'locational markers' will give a much fuller picture (Cohen & Manion, 1994, pp. 233-236)

Subjects were asked to respond to a questionnaire consisting of 10 questions. The validity of the questions was crosschecked for redundancy and for relevancy to the intent of the study by pilot-testing the questionnaire to a sample outside the actual respondents. All respondents were informed in the introductory section of the questionnaire of the intent of the study, their role in supplying valued information, and the purposes for which their information would be used.

Research Participants and the Context

Data was collected from six selected secondary schools in six major cities in six states in Nigeria (Akwa-Ibom, Cross Rivers, Delta, Edo, Enugu and Rivers state). Twelve participants, seven males and five females, agreed to take part in the study and they participated keenly. Their demographic profile revealed that they were teachers as well as head of departments in the art, sciences, and social sciences. The average age of the participants was 39 years, and their average length of service was 17 years. All participants were both academically and professionally trained and qualified as teachers. It is not uncommon for the viewpoints of a small group of teachers who have earned considerable tenure in their post to be sought for this type of study. Participants were assured of confidentiality.

Individually the participants filled out the questionnaire at a convenient time and location in the school premises. Each time, the research assistant who administered the questionnaire gave the respondents at least 30 to 45 minute intervals before collecting the completed questionnaires. The questions were close-ended, which did not allow the participants to freely express their experiences, thoughts, and feelings about their perception.

Data Analysis and Results

All data from the questionnaires were recorded and entered into a computer file for use with Statistical Package for the Social Sciences (SPSS) version 14. Analyses of data were conducted using this computer program. The Cronback Alpha reliability estimate is *0.88*, which is an acceptable value for this kind of study (Bryman & Cramer, 2001; Saunders, *et al.*, 2000).

The analyses were based on the items of the research questionnaire. The respondents were asked to check the options as they applied to them and not what they thought it should have been. The respondents were asked to rank the variables in order of the most important qualities 1, 2, 3, 4.... to the least important, such as 8, 9 and 10. Based on their responses, the variables with the least mean were taken as the most important qualities because of the value attached to them. The top ranked results revealed that a teacher should use many and varied instructional materials (m = 2.01, Sd = 1.79), a teacher should look out for children with serious personal problems (m = 2.52, Sd = 2.10), and a teacher should teach informally most of the time (m = 3.23, Sd = 2.57). The least ranked items by respondents were that a teacher should get his/her satisfaction from interest in his/her subject or from administrative work in school, rather than from classroom teaching (m = 7.25, Sd = 2.47) and a teacher should use corporal punishment (m = 8.01, Sd = 2.25) (see tables 1 for the details of the rest variables).

Discussion of Results

The use of many and varied instructional materials ranked highest in the participants' perception of their role in educational terms. Quality instructional materials are essential in teaching a particular subject. The process of selecting quality materials includes determining the degree to which they are consistent with the goals, principles, and criteria (Ngah & Masood, 2006). Similarly, teachers need to examine the ways in which the materials used in schools are deemed acceptable or good for students' development. Studies have shown that materials designed for use in schools are actually tailored to fit into teachers' pedagogical strategies (Baker & Freebody, 1989).

Teachers looking out for children with serious personal problems is one of the factors that came next to the first variable. Young children can have serious problems such as medical, social, and economic consequences that hinder their future. Whatever the issue, a teacher's job includes looking out for this type of children and giving them special attention to enhance their achievement (Armstrong, 1995).

The study revealed that teachers who teach primarily informally are results oriented and expose their students to diverse knowledge and ideas. Informal instruction calls for more social and class room interaction, which brings benefits to the students' learning process. Social interaction between teacher and students not only breaks down student isolation, but it creates an environment for students to learn in a collective and cooperative way. This in turn aids teachers to know children's individual capability and helps them develop methods towards assisting the weaker student to meet the set standards in their schools (Freiberg & Freebody, 1995).

The issue of teachers maintaining discipline at all times in school also boils down to the issue of students' compliance. In the context in which this study was carried out, various forms of power such as reward power, coercive power, position power and personal power or professional power were employed to ensure students' compliance. Unquestionably the respondents for this study ranked teachers receiving their satisfaction from interest in their subject area or from administrative work in school rather than from classroom teaching very low. The respondents ranked least the use of corporal punishment as a means for making students improve their academic achievements. Thus the role of teachers is not to use corporal punishment as a method of fostering educational development.

This research endeavor presents an effort by the researchers to make sense of the increasingly varied and complex bodies of knowledge that have become collectively known as school effectiveness and quality improvement research. The study is aimed at making contributions that might assist educational planners, policy makers, researchers, teachers, and school administrators in developing economies especially from Africa to come to terms with empirical information regarding teachers' perceptions of their attitudes and behaviors in school settings. The findings might eventually lead to a possible development or inclusion in a model of school effectiveness and quality improvement literature. The researchers found that restructuring the role of the classroom teacher as a teacher educator to facilitate the expansion of professional skills is reflective of the dynamic nature of student development (Clark, 1986; Ball & McDiarmid, 1987).

There is diversity among experienced classroom teachers in their career stages and in the personal and professional characteristics they bring to the classroom. What is appropriate for one teacher as an incentive for professional growth may not be appropriate for another. Opening an avenue of teacher growth through school-based teacher education, the classroom teacher is provided with opportunities to promote and support peer teacher growth, to experience empowerment by facilitating local change, to assume a leadership role without relinquishing the classroom, and to develop teaching behaviors which blend clinical skills with practitioner-translated research and theory. This revitalization of the teaching role with new responsibilities benefits the schooling process and its participants, and is achievable when the classroom teacher becomes a teacher educator (Bartunek, 1990). Becoming an effective teacher educator is tantamount to creating social equity in our classrooms, which means it is the duty of teachers to encourage the free pursuit of knowledge.

Table 1. Ranking of the extent to which teachers interpret their role in educational terms:

Perceived Role Variables (Locational Makers)	Rank	Mean	Std. Dev.
A teacher should use many and varied instructional materials	1	2,01	1,79
A teacher should look out for children with serious personal problems	2	2,52	2,10
A teacher should teach informally most of the time	3	3,23	2,57
A teacher should get to know children as individuals	4	3,81	2,50
A teacher should maintain discipline at all times	5	4,76	2,66
He/she should develop most of the work done in class from the children's own interests	6	5,16	2,55
A teacher should be emotionally involved with his/her pupils	7	5,69	2,38
He/she should regard scholarly attitudes to be primarily important for his/her pupils	8	6,68	2,67
A teacher should get his/her satisfaction from interest in his/her subject or from administrative work in school, rather than from classroom teaching	9	7,25	2,47
A teacher should use corporal punishment	10	8,01	2,35

References

Armstrong, D. (1995). *Power and Partnership in Education: Parent, Children and Special Educational Needs*. London and New York: Routledge.

Austin, H., Dwyer, B. & Freebody, P. (2003). *Schooling the Child: The Making of Students in Classrooms*. London: Routledge Falmer.

Baker, C. D. & Freebody, P. (1989). Children's First School Books: Introduction to the Challenges in Beginning School Reading Books. *Australia Journal of Reading*, Vol. 11(2), pp. 95-104.

Ball, D. L., and McDiarmid, G. W. (1987). Understanding how Teaching Knowledge Changes. *NCRTE Colloquy*, pp. 9-11.

Bartunek, H. M. (1990). The Classroom Teacher as Teacher Educator. ERIC Clearinghouse on Teacher Education Washington DC.

Bryman, A. & Cramer, D. (2001). *Quantitative Data Analysis for Social Scientists*. London: Routledge

Campbell, J., Kyriakides, L., Muijs, D. & Robinson, W. (2004). *Assessing Teacher Effectiveness: Developing a Differentiated Model*. London: RoutledgeFalmer.

Cheng, Y. C. (1994) Classroom Environment and Student affective Performance: An effective Profile. *Journal of Experimental Education*, Vol. 62 Issue 3, pp. 221-239.

Cheng, Y. C., Cheung, W. M. & Tam, W. M. (2002) "The Pacific Rim and Australia" - Hong Kong. In Reynolds, D., Creemers, B., Stringfield, S., Teddlie, C. and Schaffer, G. (Eds) *World Class Schools: International Perspectives on School Effectiveness*. London: RoutledgeFalmer. pp. 138-155.

Clark, C. (1986). "Ten Years of Conceptual Development in Research on Teacher Thinking". In M. Ben-Perez, R. Bromme & R. Halkes (Eds), *Advances of Research on Teacher Thinking*. Lisse: Swets & Zeitlinger. pp. 7-20.

Clark, D. L. (1986). "Transforming the structure for the professional preparation of teachers". In J. D. Raths and L. G. Katz (Eds.), *Advances in Teacher Education*, Vol. 2, pp. 1-19. Norwood, NJ: Ablex.

Cohen, L. & Manion, L. (1994). *Research Methods in Education* 4th Edition. London and New York: Routledge.

Creemers, B. P. M. (1994) *The Effective Classroom*. London: Caseell.

Cushman, K. (1998). Teacher Renewal: Essential in a Time of Change. *Horace*. Vol. 14, (4).

Eraut, M. (1994): *Development Professional Knowledge and Competence*. London: Falmer Press.

Freiberg, J. & Freebody, P. (1995). Analyzing Literacy Events in the Classroom and Homes: Conversation-Analysis Approaches. In Freebody, P., Ludwig, and Gunn, S. (Eds) *Everyday Literacy Practices in and Out of School in Low Socio-economic Urban Communities*, Vol. 1, Report to the Commonwealth of Employment, Education and Training, Melbourne: Curriculum Corporation, pp. 185-376.

Golembiewski, R. T. (1973). Motivation. In Carl Heyel (Ed.), *The Encyclopedia of Management* 2nd. New York: Van Nostrand Reinhold.

Hämäläinen, S. and Jokela, J. (Eds) (1993) *Summary of Case Studies: Quality in Teaching*. University of Jyväskylä, Department of Teacher Education. Research 54.

Hardre, P. L. & Reeve, J. (2003). A Motivational Model of Rural Students' Intentions to Persist In, Versus Drop Out, of High School, *Journal of Educational Psychology*, Vol. 95, 2, pp. 347-356.

Hoy, W. K. & Miskel, C. G. (1987). *Educational Administration: Theory, Research and Practice.* New York: Random House.

Husu, J. (2003). Constructing Ethical Representations From the Teacher's Pedagogical Practice: A Case of Prolonged Reflection. *Interchange* Vol. 34(1), pp. 1-21.

Husu, J. (2006). Analyzing Teachers' Rule-based Competencies in Practice. Paper Presented at the European conference on Educational Research (ECER). Held in Geneva, Switzerland September 13-16, 2006.

Ifinedo, P. (2004). *Motivation and Job Satisfaction among Information Systems Developers- Perspectives from Finland, Nigeria and Estonia*: A Preliminary Study. In Vasilecas, O., Caplinskas, A., Wojtkowski, W., Wojtkowski, W. G., Zupancic, J. and Wryczw, S. (Eds.), Proceedings of the 13th. International Conference on Information Systems Development: Advances in Theory, Practice Methods, and Education, 9 - 11 September, 2004, Vilnius, Lithuania, pp. 161 -172.

Jenkins, J. M. (1999). Teaching for Tomorrow the Changing Role of Teachers in the Connected Classroom. EDEN 1999 Open Classroom Conference — Balatonfüred. Retrieved 20/06/07 from http://www.eden-online.org/papers/jenkins.pdf#search=%22teachers%20classroom%20roles%22

Kelly, J. (1974). *Organizational Behavior.* Homewood: Richard D. Irwin.

Lewis, P. S., Goodman, S. H. & Fandt, P. M. (1995). *Management: Challenges in the 21st Century.* New York: West Publishing Company.

Lumsden, L. S. (1994). Student Motivation to Learn. *Eric Clearinghouse on educational Management.*

Ngah, N. A. & Masood, M. (2006). Development of ICT Instructional Materials Based on Needs Identified by Malaysia Secondary School Teachers. Proceedings of the 2006 Informing Science and IT Education Joint Conference Salford, UK — June 25-28

Niederhauser, J. S. (1997). Motivating Learners at the South Korean University. *Forum.* Vol. 35(1).

Ololube, N. P. (2005a). "Benchmarking the Motivational Competencies of Academically Qualified Teachers and Professionally Qualified Teachers in Nigerian Secondary Schools". *The African Symposium,* Vol. 5(3), pp. 17-37.

Ololube, N. P. (2005b). "School Effectiveness and Quality Improvement: Quality Teaching in Nigerian Secondary Schools". *The African Symposium,* Vol. 5(4), pp. 17-31.

Raffini, J. (1993). *Winners Without Losers: Structures and Strategies for Increasing Student Motivation to Learn.* Boston: Allyn and Bacon.

Reynolds, D. (1994). Preface and Introduction. In Reynolds, D., Creemers, B. P. M., Nesseelrodt, P. S., Schaffer, E. C., Stringfield, S. and Tedelie, C. (Eds).

Advances *in School Effectiveness Research and Practice*. Willington: Elsevier Science. pp. 1-6.
Rosenfield, R. H. & Wilson, D. C. (1999). *Managing Organizations: Text, Readings and Cases*, London: McGraw-Hill.
Saunders, M., Lewis, P., and Thornhill, A. (2000). *Research Methods for Business* Studies, (2nd) Edition. Harlow: Printice Hall.
Shulman, L. S. (1986). Those who understand: Knowledge growth in teaching. *Educational Researcher, 15,* 4-14.

Shulman, L. S. (1987). Knowledge and teaching: Foundations of the new reform. *Harvard Educational Review, 57,* 1-22.
Tharp, R. & Gallimore, R. (1998). A Theory of Teaching as Assisted Performance. In Faulkner, D., Littleton, K. and Woodhead, M. (Eds) *Learning Relationships in the Classroom*. London: Routledge and The Open University, 94-110.
UNESCO (2001). Teacher Education through Distance Education. Paris. UNESCO.
UNESCO (2002). Information and Communication Technologies in Teacher education: A Planning Guide. Paris. UNESCO.
Vygotsky, L.S. (1978). *Mind and society: The development of higher mental processes*. Cambridge, MA: Harvard University Press.

Rethinking Equal Voices In Classroom Discourse: Arab Female College Students' Views on Literacy Empowerment

Negmeldin O. Alsheikh
United Arab Emirates University, UAE

Introduction

This study aimed at investigating the views of female college students from United Arab Emirates University on literacy and empowerment. It looks at the creation of equal voices in classroom practices and explores the students' views on literacy as they relate to empowerment with reference to literacy and sociolinguistic concepts of the dialogical self. The study is inspired by the Russian literary scholar Mikhail Bakhtin. Central to Bakhtin's theory is the idea of the dialogical-self which considers an individual's identity as multivoiced, multiliterate, and dialogical, which acknowledges the role of human interchange and the impact of power in social relations. The theory of the dialogical self helped us to understand how United Arab Emirates University female students, at the college of education mediate their views on literacy, cultural identity and power with respect to their understanding of what makes an individual powerful and literate.

New trends in literacy education viewed learning as situated activity which has as its central defining characteristic a process that Lave & Wenger (1991) call "legitimate peripheral participation" (p. 29). We can view the legitimate peripheral participation as a source to speak about different relations as they relate to knowledge communities and practice in a dialogical sense (Lave & Wenger, 1991). Dialogue is a fundamental approach to pedagogy; its different forms enable students to explore deeper assumptions about epistemology, the nature of communication, cultural practices, and the roles of teacher and learner (Luke, 2006; Gee, 1996; Barton, 1994; Cazden, 1988).

The Site of Meaning and Power

The rethinking of dialogue is shaped by a long tradition which regards all communicative and representational acts as forms of social practice (Cazden, 1988; Foucault, 1972, 1980; Gee, 1996; Luke, 2006). This tradition explores discourses as forms of socio-historically constituted relations among people, activities, texts, and situations (Fendler & Tuckey, 2006).

Some researchers, called for sociology of social inequality which may provide us with a wider scope for modeling differences that exist among groups of people, where one group is more advantaged than another. For example, the disadvantageous position of illiterates is not equated with fundamentally other forms of similar disadvantage, such as disabilities, ethnic minorities, gender inequality, or being a child of unskilled manual workers (Payne, 2006).

Paulo Freire (1968) advanced the metaphor of traditional literacy as banking where knowledge is deposited in empty vessels (Freire and Macedo, 1987; Friere, 1968). To clarify the ways that can shape and empower life Giroux (1993) emphasizes that literacy neither a skill nor knowledge, but is "an emerging act of conscious resistance" (p. 367). Freire & Macedo (1987) advance the idea that "every reading of the word is preceded by reading of the world" (p. 58). The relationship between reading and empowerment is well documented in research (see Smith, 2004). In a lettered society, it is more likely that those who cannot read and write are at disadvantages (Smith, 2004). It was an understanding of literacy function in society that can give individuals voices by putting literacy into use, this view is also supported by the classical work of Heath (1983) and Street (1984).

Self and Others

The dialogical principles that addressed the cultural and literacy system developed by Bakhtin (1981, 1986, 1993) are of great importance to our view of a literate worldview, especially when we look at the intimate and yet complex relationships that surrounded the self and others. Culture in a sense, has an ultimate role, besides forming the mind, "its individual expression inheres in meaning making" (Bruner, 1996, p. 3).

For the purposes of this research the different positions held by the female college students who are situated in Arab and Islamic culture are important to our understanding of a multi-layered and multi-voiced self that Bakhtin talks about. The aim of our interpretation, therefore, is to arrive at an understanding of the dialogical argument which may suggest that the language the participants use in this exchange embeds the meanings and significations that the participants attach in their responses to particular questions that were directed to them.

Analysis

According to Glaser and Strauss (1967), who first developed the constant comparative analysis and was later refined by Lincoln and Guba (1985), the constant comparative method is concerned with generating and plausibly suggesting many categories, properties, and hypotheses about general problems. The authors describe four stages for executing the constant comparative method; these are: 1. comparing incidents applicable to each category, 2. integrating categories and their properties, 3. delimiting the theory, and 4. writing the theory (Glaser & Strauss, 1967, p. 105). To analyze the data that emerged, the researcher was assisted by two research assistants to make sure there was agreement about instances of occurrences of the views that participants share. This was done in three stages, we first analyzed data for the occurrences, in the second stage we integrated categories and their properties with units change from comparison of incidents and in the third step, we formulated a smaller set of categorical concepts, and the fourth stage involved providing the content behind the categories.

The participants of this study were 30 undergraduate female college of Education students from United Arab Emirates University. The mean age of the participants was 22 years. Geographically, the participants came from the seven different Emirates (states) which constitute the union of the country. They also represent varying socioeconomic status. To elicit different responses from the participants, general questions were asked which reflected issues pertaining to the individual-self and its function in the society; importance of literacy to their personality, important things that literacy and their characters as females in the society, being equal to males as a result of gaining literacy abilities, empowerment of literacy to share ideas in the classroom, and the support of literacy for their voices to be heard in the class and in the society at large. We used the concept of voice here as a methodological tool, as metaphoric mean which indicates the fact that what is written here does not reflect language in its strict structural sense but the use of language to convey meanings that reflect the speaking subject's concepts, perspectives and worldviews.

The Literate Self and Others

We explored the written responses by means of the concepts of voices (dialogism) to analyze the two facets of self identity. While we see self identity concepts as partly cross classifying and overlapping, we nevertheless argue that these voices have a potential to depict and capture the self construction and hence the representational facets of self identity. The ways of self expression and the self constructing of relationships with others are not determined only by the responses but also by the reflections of the participants' self identities as they were depicted by the concept of voice. The emerging themes that follow the analysis illustrate the relatedness of the individual self to the social group. In general we came to the conclusion that there were four recurring and emerging themes. The first two themes were related to how the participants see themselves in terms of 1. self situating and self-positing in a given context; 2. self reflection which refers to the view of the self enacted within a given context. The other two themes are related to the view of self versus others in societal setting; 3. authority, which refers to the idea of possessing a central voice to talk of change and in an authoritative voice; 4. confrontational which refers to the idea of speaking in resilient voices.

In a very important sense, these written responses could be looked upon in terms of a narrative of personal views. What is said here in the emerging interaction draws on the discourses of the individual self with others in the society. The represented or constructed self is connected with the phenomenal world of the participants' life in their society.

Self-Situating and Self-Reflections

In this part we explored how the UAE University female college students positioned themselves in their social and learning contexts mediated by literacy. We also explored their self-reflection on literacy act and learning. In general almost all of them have a positive view of how literacy empowers and liberates them, as the following examples demonstrate:

> Shamsa: "I think literacy adds to me personally several things which made me a person with an important role in the society. For example, without literacy and learning I will not develop these abilities or I will not have any role in my society. It also allows me to be more independent in my thinking and to have an equal role and rights as men do."

> Fatima: "Literacy helps me to understand other people's opinions, which in turn allows me to think and to understand what is happening in the world today. I read books, newspapers and in the internet. Also, writing abilities helped me to state my opinions and interact and exchange information with other people. Sometimes, writing helps me to remember what I want to say when I present information. Literacy in general helps when I discuss issues."

> Alia: "I can say that literacy adds to my character many things such as knowledge and it makes me a strong person to talk about many issues I want to talk about. It also gives me confidence by being aware of what I am taking about, and it also provides me with awareness."

Reflection on Literacy

The participants also reflected on their educational experience. They compared the new literate generations of today and the generations of the past, they also made comparison between females and males in the society, and they also talked about literacy as it liberates and emancipates and bring female's voices to the front. The participants envisioned new positive roles for UAE women today as compared to the past; they see women today as having great roles in the society than in the past. In terms of gender equality, most of them see a complementary relationship in which men are more competitive in some types of jobs and women in others. Nonetheless, some of them see men as more practical and women are too emotional. But overall some of them see themselves sometimes surpassing males in their society and creating for themselves voices and important roles in the society. Here are some examples which illustrate that:

> Noura: "Literacy adds a lot to me as a female in the society because in the past in the UAE as you know that women only stay at home and they can't work and communicate with aliens. Also, the females didn't always complete their schooling, but now the educated women have effects on the society. On the other hand, literate and educated females will be able to raise their children better, which helps the child to become a better member in the society."

> Mariam: "I don't belief in equality between men and women, because they have different nature; a man and a woman complete one another there is no one better than the other. Both women and men have special things. So, literacy is important and it benefits the society. It also affects females' critical thinking and it helps them to have control over their life. From my own experiences I know that females are more emotional than males."

> Sahikha: "I don't think men and women are equal because everyone has his own character, knowledge, personality and responsibility. There are many things that a woman can be better at such as being a nurse. On the other hand, there are some jobs that only men can do such as working as a mechanic or a builder. A woman can't work as mechanic in the UAE."

> Zainab: "Of course, literacy makes women open to all different aspects of life and this is what happened to me. I am now able to work as a man, and I am able to overcome difficult matters. Education grants us more useful knowledge through our majors in college. We aspire to expand the child's mental faculties and empower him or her. Literacy enables me to be capable of thinking clearly and it allows me to go beyond the limits of my emotion."

Resilient Voices

Although most of the participants believed that literacy enabled them to possess a positive voice for change, still some others were not sure if their voices would be heard. In addition, some of them made a comparison between themselves as literate females with other illiterate ones, and yet some others compared themselves to males. In all of that they believed that they were better than illiterate females and that they were competing with men in all domains because they possess literacy abilities. The participants held a belief that literacy empowered them to have a voice in their society, while few of them thought that females' voices are still subdued and unacceptable. The following examples illustrate that:

> Laila: "Literacy supports my voice gradually especially in our society which considers our voices as a last resort. Still, it remains valid and considerable. At

the classroom level, being literate helps me to speak without being shy and without being afraid of the authorities, of course in good manner. It also enhances my self-esteem because I can verbalize my thoughts."

Sarah: "I believe that I am strong than other females who didn't come to the university or who didn't have a chance to study in any school. I have much information than them and I can discuss different affairs in a scientific way. Also, my values are higher than theirs in our society."

Shaima: "Females may not be able to be like men in all kinds of knowledge and learning but what we see now in the education evolution and the tendency of most women to make change in their thinking... I realized that women have the capacity to become counterparts to men and particularly what we see now where the number of graduates from men's side is increasing."

Amnah: "A literate female understands the reality of life from pains, fights and sufferings. She also knows what her rights, what is unjust and who are the oppressed. Literacy makes you aware about what happen in real life. It also makes you think about positive changes and built a strong character and it gives you self-confidence and self-esteem and it further makes me open to other cultures and to the world."

Salma: "I think that women are not only equal to men, but they are better than them sometimes in terms of the abilities that women have. Of course literacy empowered me because it helped me to share some responsibilities with other members of the society. It also helped me to be more confident in myself and flexible in my ideas with others. It further motivated me to know my rights and duties in the society."

Confrontational Voices

One meeting point between the individual and the social milieu was the position of these females in a society. The perspective that these females seemed to assume here was confrontational in the sense that they spoke about their place in the society as compared to men. The focus of females' voices in this part was on the striving for potential empowerment. Although most of them believed that literacy added a lot to them and made them stand in equal footing with males, yet others spoke in daring and confrontational voices as they saw their voices should be taken in account vis-à-vis males' voices. The following examples depict that:

Rehab: "Literacy abilities can make me equal to men and sometimes better than men. Because sometimes the ideas that woman generate are stronger than those of men. I think sometimes women's abilities of thinking are better than those of men. For example, women's thinking leads them to solve problems better than men. In addition, literacy abilities can make women competing with men in the society when they express and share their ideas in many fields as men do."

Shama: "Literacy plays an important role in shaping my personality. Reading increases my knowledge and my experiences in life. It also motivates me to deal with people and discuss with them some issues. This discussion gives me confidence and a trust on my self. It also gives me self respect and respect to other people's opinions. On the other hand, writing helps me to express my opinions and it enables me to discover my weakness and potentials. I can now defend my rights and other people' rights through writing."

Shama: "Having literacy abilities helps me to have an important role in my society. I can also prove for men how I can become equal to them by studying hard. Moreover, it gives me the power to say my opinion freely because I am an educated person graduating from the university. Furthermore, I can do many good things for my country by contributing in its progress, by sharing my ideas and by participating in some events or conferences."

Waffa: "Naturally, uneducated people have a low confidence in participating and sharing their ideas than the educated ones. Before having literacy abilities I don't like to share my opinions in the classroom because I thought that if I made a mistake people are going to laugh at me. After having good education I have trust on myself and on my opinions and I can say my opinion out loud without any fear because I learned something from experiences that all people will learn from their mistakes. So, my advice to others is you can make mistakes and say you opinion whatever it is to learn."

Conclusions

We discussed a case study in which we analyzed the views of female college students from the United Arab Emirates University on literacy and empowerment. We looked at the creation of equal voices in classroom practices and explored the students' views on literacy as they relate to culture identity, empowerment with reference to literacy and sociolinguistic concepts of the dialogical self. I argued that we can explore the relations between the subjective-self and the social objectivity by looking at classroom discourse as it generates consciousness through social practices. Further, we looked at participants as they interacted exclusively in their social milieu and recognized them as agents who were able, to an extent, to appropriate discourses and build a perspective of their own that has both continuous and constantly renegotiated qualities.

Finally, as to the manifestations of the UAE female college students' views on literacy and empowerment, the way these students talked about literacy and empowerment in this case study was a multifaceted interplay of their positions as females and literate beings in a male dominant society. Their voices bear a strong sense of the awareness of the social and historical factors that shaped the traditional ways of looking at women. At the same time, they expressed a confident view of the future. They were also confident that their education would be passed on to the future generations and that literacy would play a decisive role in this.

References

Bakhtin, M. (1981). *The Dialogic Imagination: Four Essays*. M. Holquist (Ed.), C. Emerson & M. Holquist (Trans). Austin, Texas: University of Texas Press.

Bakhtin, M. (1986). *Speech Genres and Other Late Essays*. C. Emerson & M. Holquist (Eds.), V. W. McGee (Trans.). Austin, Texas: University of Texas Press.

Bakhtin, M. (1993). *Toward a philosophy of the act*. M. Holquist (Ed.), V. Liapunov (Tr.). Austin, Texas : University of Texas Press.

Barton, D. (1994). *Literacy: An introduction to the ecology of written language*. Oxford, Ox, Blackwell Publishers Ltd.

Bruner, J. (1996). *The Culture of Education*. Cambridge, Massachusetts: Harvard University Press.

Cazden, C. B. (1988). *Classroom discourse: The language of teaching and learning*. Portsmouth, NH: Heinemann.

Fendler, L. & Tuckey, S. F. (2006). "Whose Literacy? Discursive constructions of life and objectivity." *Educational Philosophy and Theory* 38 (5), 589 — 606.

Foucault, M. (1972). *The archaeology of knowledge and the discourse on language* (trans. A. M. Sheridan Smith). New York: Pantheon Books.

Foucault, M. (1980). *Power/knowledge: Selected interviews and other writings 1972-1977*. New York: Pantheon Books.

Freire, P. (1968). *The pedagogy of the oppressed* (M. B. Ramos, Trans.). New York: Seabury.

Freire, P. & Macedo, D. (1987). *Literacy: Reading the word and the world*. Massachusetts: Bergin & Garvey.

Gee, J. P. (1996). *Social linguistics and literacies: Ideology in discourses* (2nd Ed). London: The Falmer Press.

Giroux, H. (1993). "Literacy and the politics of difference." In C. Lankshear & P. Mclaren (Eds.), *Critical literacy: Politics, praxis, and postmodernism* (pp. 367-377). Albany, NY: State University of New York Press.

Glaser, B.G., & Strauss, A.L. (1967). *The discovery of grounded theory: Strategies for qualitative research*. Chicago, IL: Aldine.

Lave, J., & Wenger, E. (1991). *Situated Learning: Legitimate Peripheral Participation*. Cambridge, England: Cambridge University Press.

Lincoln, Y. S., and Guba, E.G. (1985). *Naturalistic inquiry*. Beverly Hills, CA: Sage.

Payne, G. (2006) "Re-counting 'illiteracy': literacy skills in the sociology of social inequality." *The British Journal of Sociology*, 57 (2), 219 —240.

Smith, V. (2004). "Empowering teachers: empowering children? How can researchers initiate and research empowerment?" *Journal of Research in Reading* 27 (4), 413 —424.

Street, B. (1984). *Literacy in theory and practice*. Cambridge: Cambridge University Press.

About the Authors

Negmeldin Omer Alsheikh is an assistant Professor in the United Arab Emirates University. He is specialized in Literacy Education; his interests is in reading, L1 and L2 learning and teaching, language acquisition, meta-cognitive reading and discourses in language.

Hala Al-Yamani is at the Faculty of Education at Bethlehem University. Her research focuses on the role of drama in initial teacher education and particularly the use of drama in the Early Childhood Teacher Education programs at Bethlehem University. In addition, she has worked with the Ministry of Education and other International foundations such as Save the Children and UNICEF in planning and training programs for trainers and supervisors of the Early Childhood stage. She has worked with the Curriculum Department at the Ministry of Education on evaluating the Drama Curriculum for the first five classes which was developed by a group of teachers and supervisors.

Daniel Elemchuku Egbezor is a Senior Lecturer and Head of Department in the Department of Educational Foundations at the University of Port Harcourt, Nigeria. He has written extensively in the areas of school effectiveness, teacher education, and curriculum reforms and has presented in national and international conferences. His publications have appeared in national and international journals, including chapters in books.

Hala Elhoweris is assistant professor of Special Education at United Arab Emirates University. Her research interests include educating students with disabilities in general education classes, meeting the needs of students from culturally and linguistically diverse backgrounds and gifted and talented students.

Ponni Iyer is Senior Lecturer at Guru Nanak College of Education and Research, Mumbai, India. She completed her M.Ed. and M.Phil while serving as school teacher for 13 years before moving on to work as a teacher educator. She has completed 17 years as a teacher educator and is now pursuing doctoral studies. She is visiting faculty for postgraduate teaching at the University of Mumbai and has presented papers at National and International conferences including UNESCO (Adelaide, Australia, 2004).

About the Authors

Themina Kader, since 1994, when she first came to the United States of America, has been involved in the pedagogy of art education at all levels. Teaching both undergraduate and graduate students how to teach art, and how to promote the concepts of multiculturalism and diversity in all its permutation is the raison d'être of her professional career. Toward that end she has written fairly widely in art education journals at national and international levels.

Govinda Ishwar Lingam is a Senior Lecturer in Primary Education at the School of Education, University of the South Pacific, Suva, Fiji. His research interests include issues relating to equity in education, professional development of teachers, values education, teacher-education and educational

Thomas Muhr holds a German teaching degree, two British master degrees and is completing his ESRC-funded PhD in the Centre for Globalisation, Education & Societies, University of Bristol (UK). He has worked in secondary and tertiary, formal and non-formal educational institutions in diverse socio-economic settings in Europe and Latin America. Currently, Thomas researches different aspects of the contemporary Latin American revolutionary processes, with a particular focus on Venezuela's Higher Education For All, social justice and human rights within the democratic socialist development model and its regionalisation and globalisation as the Bolivarian Alternative for the Peoples of our America (ALBA).

Nwachukwu Prince Ololube is a Lecturer 1 in the Department of Educational Foundations and Management, University of Education, Port Harcourt, Nigeria. He has written extensively in the areas of institutional management and leadership, school effectiveness, teacher effectiveness and quality improvement, and ICT in education. He has published in various international journals, chapters in books, and leading international conference proceedings.

Gowri Parameswaran obtained her Bachelors in psychology from Mumbai University and her Masters and Doctoral degrees from Rutgers University in New Jersey. She teaches classes on the foundations of education, especially the psychological aspects of learning. Her other teaching expertise includes topics in women's studies and multicultural education. She is currently serving as chairperson in the department of Educational Studies in the School of Education at SUNY New Paltz. She has published peer-reviewed articles and book chapters on various issues pertaining to diversity and social justice in education. She is currently co-editing a book about the barriers facing the education of the marginalized in several developing countries.

About the Authors

Mary Thornton is the Assistant Director of Learning and Teaching in Centre for the Enhancement of Learning and Teaching (CELT) in the University of Hertfordshire. She received her Ph, D. in 1992, and MA 1984 from University of London. She has published articles and book chapters in the area of gender and culture in education. She is a member of the of Higher Education Academy in the British Educational Research Association.

Cory Young is an Assistant Professor of Communication Management and Design in the Department of Strategic Communication at Ithaca College. Her research interests include the scholarship of teaching and learning, sexuality, gender, and organizational communication. She is committed to being a social just educator, by raising awareness of critical issues that students face.

www.ingramcontent.com/pod-product-compliance
Lightning Source LLC
Chambersburg PA
CBHW021834300426
44114CB00009BA/434